RETIRE EARLY

RETIRE EARLY

What Are You Waiting For?

by

Eric Gaddy

LIONESS PRESS

Hendersonville, NC

IP

Lioness Press
PO Box 928
Hendersonville, NC 28793

Lioness Press books may be purchased for educational, business, or sales promotional use. For information, please email the Special Markets Department at info@lionesspress.us.

FIRST EDITION

Designed by W. Anne Jones
Cover design by Cassandra Bowen, Uzuri Designs

LCCN 2018938687

ISBN 978-1-948922-00-5

Manufactured in the United States of America

10 9 8 7 6 5 4 3 2 1

To my children Kate and Frank. I am so proud of the young woman and young man that you have become.

To my life partner, Deb. I have never felt so loved in my life. Adventure awaits us my love.

To my sister Lisa. Thank you for being my protector when we were children. I wish Carol was with us, so she could read the book.

CONTENTS

Introduction

We have been sold a bill of goods. I bought the bill and, most likely, you have as well. I bet if you look around at your friends and family, they have too. Generation after generation has fallen into the same set of circumstances, most not even aware that they are in it. So, what is this bill of goods we have been sold?

After we graduate from high school, we all choose one of three directions: We're either going to college, going to the military, or going to work. At some point, most of us are going to meet that special someone, fall in love, get married, and have babies. Once the kids are out of high school and ready to start their own lives, we are probably in our mid-forties. We look up and say, "I'm forty-five years old. Boy, retirement at sixty-five is *only* twenty years away. That's not so far off."

So, you get to age sixty-five and retire. If you're lucky, you have ten good years to travel and do the things you always talked about doing: see the Grand Canyon, spend time in Costa Rica, ride your Harley Davidson across America, and so on.

In an ideal world, you planned your early retirement years ago and the fruits of your frugality, savings, and planning have come to market. You sacrificed living in the biggest house in the neighborhood or driving some brand-new car every two years to save toward your goal of early retirement. Now it's time to put your retiring early plan into motion.

As a financial advisor for over twenty-four years, I love working with people, clients, and prospective clients. However, over the past couple years, I have become unhappy with the financial industry. If I could focus on my clients 100 percent of the time, life would be great. But the industry has changed, increasing regulations of FINRA and the SEC have resulted in additional paperwork. More of my time has been taken away from client contact. Like many people who have worked in the same industry for the past twenty years, whether it be a doctor, lawyer, or some other industry, doing business is a lot harder these days than when we first started our careers.

I became disenchanted. So, if you are unhappy in your career, I doubt if your disdain for your job crept up overnight. Normally, the seeds of unhappiness in your career have been planted for some time. I feel like I have accomplished everything I set out to do in my career, but when my seeds were planted and grew, I knew it was time to pursue a different path.

I've met with over eight thousand couples and individuals during my career. Ninety-nine percent of the time when I'm discussing a couple's retirement plan, they have set a retirement age as a goal. Ninety percent of the time that age is sixty-five.

Why do folks focus on an age to be retired by? Why has the age sixty-five become the default age for most people? Two reasons: One reason is that for many years to get your full social security payment, you had to wait until age sixty-five. Another reason is that at age sixty-five, you can apply for Medicare. Both social security and Medicare are targets to reach—social security gives us guaranteed income and Medicare gives us healthcare benefits. For decades, those two items gave people the peace of mind they needed to move into retirement.

Now, I can understand why people associate retirement at sixty-five due to social security and Medicare, but I think people fall into the trap of "this is what society expects and this is the way it is supposed to be."

When you meet someone who tells you they just retired and they're fifty-two years old, the first thing that pops into your mind is probably, "They're rich." Perhaps, you think they have a health issue that forced them to retire early. These are natural conclusions because retiring at fifty-two years old is not the norm. Many people associate retirement with folks in their sixties—not in their forties or fifties. With this book, I want to reset your thinking regarding retirement. Retirement should not be based on age.

Webster's defines retirement as "withdrawal from one's position or occupation or from active working life." This is how many people define what retirement is and how we look at it. My definition is a bit different. I define retirement as "Withdrawal from one's career to gain freedom and control of one's life in which you may continue to work, yet only on what, when, and what pace you wish."

Growing up, my family's business was a funeral home, which had been in our family for over eighty years. At eight years old, I helped my mom move dead bodies. Heck, I thought every eight-year-old was doing this. (It's amazing what you can get used to.) Throughout my time helping at the mortuary, I saw young babies who didn't survive, kids my own age dead, as well as teenagers, young men and women in their twenties and thirties, all the way up to folks over 100 years old. When I left home for college, there were two major themes that I carried with me: life is short, and I know my time is running out. We all know we're going to die but most people won't give that much thought or choose not to think about it. But as I grow older, I think about it and now I want to make the most of my time.

In my office, I have a picture of me (about ten years old) and two girls about the same age. Growing up, I remember playing with the girls in the backyard. I keep the picture in my office to remind me how precious life is: one of the girls died around age eleven from a horse riding accident and the other young girl died in her twenties from muscular dystrophy. I never really knew my father, but I understand he died at age fifty-two. I lost a sister a few years ago at age fifty-one and lost my former business partner a couple years ago at age forty-seven.

About a year ago, I had a true awakening. I surveyed the friends and family I've lost over the years, and I looked at how society expects people to work until they are sixty-five years old, which only leaves them with a short window of time to enjoy their freedom. I researched how people were retiring early and how they were successful at it. Some folks retired early because, indeed, they were rich, or they did have health issues. However, many folks have retired in their fifties, and they are *not* wealthy. They are average, healthy women and men who were tired of the day-in, day-out schedule

MY REASONS FOR EARLY RETIREMENT

Have you contemplated early retirement? Included here are my top six reasons for retiring early. What are yours?

1. Yes, get out of the rat race. I'm just tired of the corporate world.
2. Freedom. Do what I want, when I want.
3. Life is short. My dad, who I never really knew, died at fifty-two. My grandfather died at sixty-four. Living a long life is not part of my genetics.
4. Buck the trend. As a retirement planning specialist, I witnessed society almost force people to look at sixty-five as the age of retirement. If there is a trend that says you must go this way, I generally go the opposite way.
5. See the world. Endless work prevents me from traveling the globe. I don't want to wait until I'm seventy years old sporting an oxygen tank while climbing the Great Wall of China. I want to see and view the world as a younger man.
6. Live by example. I want to show others that retiring early can be done.

So, what are you waiting for?

of working 9-to-5, Monday through Friday, collecting a paycheck, spending that paycheck over the weekend, only to do it again when Monday rolled around. Perhaps you can relate?

Trading Freedom for Money

Would you pay $1,000,000 for twenty extra years of your life? If we knew that we could get that for certain, we'd probably beg, borrow, and steal to find $1,000,000. Think about it in another way. If you make $50,000 a year, over twenty years, that is $1,000,000. Keep in mind, you won't keep the full $1,000,000 because Uncle Sam is going to take a good portion of that for taxes. Is twenty years of your freedom worth $1,000,000? For some folks, the answer would be *absolutely not*, and they'll keep chugging away at work. For others, they would gladly trade the money for their freedom.

What is your freedom worth to you? Freedom to come and go as you please. Freedom from that cubicle that will entrap you if you allow it. Freedom to live life on your terms versus someone else's. You have the power to break free, not just from your career but from the way you think. Our brains can become our prison. The way we think has been shaped by our parents at an early age as well as television, media, and society. When you start thinking for yourself independently of others, something powerful starts awakening inside you. You start viewing the world with different lenses. You free yourself from society's expectations. You find out that it's okay to be a little selfish and do the things that make you happy. You realize you can break through barriers and leave behind what's holding you back. And, most important, when you start thinking for yourself, independently of others, you take control of your own life.

If not, then your career will keep you occupied and trapped for as long as you let it. Television and media will have you buying stuff that anchors you down. Societal pressures make you fall in line and follow a certain path—one that makes you consume, consume, consume. Do

CONSUMERISM

Consumerism is the pressure to purchase and consume goods. Ever since the invention of radio, television, magazines, and now the Internet, generations of Americans have been bombarded by ads to purchase goods they couldn't "live without." Whether it was a seductive ad or 24-hour shopping networks, marketing firms figured out what appealed to our senses and played them. The result? We have a bunch of stuff that we "had to have," which now clutters our homes.

you own your possessions or do your possessions own you?

It's time to turn things around. You need to trade money to be free. Buy back your time. Start thinking of your own freedom and what that would mean to you. Listen, we are all going to die. Hopefully, not for many years but that's not a guarantee. Wake up and start living, otherwise you're only going through the motions every day and you're dying a slow death at work.

Remember, you are in control of your own life. Are you ready to get a plan and focus on your early retirement or will you maintain the status quo and keep doing the same thing repeatedly? You have a choice, and I'm going to show you how to successfully retire on your terms.

The first part of this book is where I teach you how to retire early. We'll look at your financial numbers and discuss the steps you need to take to be prepared to retire.

In Part Two, we'll talk about two of the biggest worries on everyone's minds: healthcare and social security. How will early retirement affect your healthcare and your social security?

In Part Three, we'll look at different lifestyles younger retirees are flocking toward, such as expats living in foreign countries, mobile lifestyles, and simplified living.

And, in the end, I'll give you my own plan for retirement. Throughout, numerous tips and tools will guide you on the path to retirement.

Are you ready?

Get set, retire....

PART ONE

D.I.A.L.
into Early Retirement

etiring early requires a lot of planning. You must get your finances in order. The four core financial areas are: (D)ebt, (I)ncome, (A)ssets, and (L)ifestyle. I created D.I.A.L. because it's simple and to the point. These four areas are crucial when deciding to retire, whether you want to retire early or at age sixty-five. These areas decide how well you are set up for a successful early retirement, so take control of each one and you are off and running in retirement regardless of your age.

DEBT

Debt crashes the dreams of retiring early for many folks. I can look back today and see the multiple mistakes I made with debt over my lifetime. It started when I was a full-time student in college with only a part-time job. I was twenty years old, and Mastercard and Visa would send me credit card applications offering me a $1000 to $2000 credit limit. What twenty-year-old wouldn't want to be able to buy what they

> **KNOW YOUR FINANCIAL NUMBERS**
> Ask yourself these questions:
>
> - How much debt do I have?
> - How much income do I have?
> - How much are my assets worth?
> - How much does my lifestyle cost?

want, when they wanted it? That was the first of many mistakes. Up until ten years ago, I bought a new car or truck every few years not paying attention to the depreciation hit I was taking every time I traded and, remember, I'm a financial advisor who should know better.

Debt is like eating, it's fun to eat anything you want, but it's not so fun to diet to drop the pounds. The instant gratification of a new $5000+ limit credit card or a brand-new car is exhilarating, but it can present problems to your wallet.

INCOME

One thing for certain, we all need income to survive, whether that income comes from a job, pension, investments, rental properties, social security, or a disability check. Without income, our options are very limited and retiring early is not possible.

So, you need income to retire early. Where does that income come from?

If you retired from your career early, don't have a pension, and are too young for social security, then your income might need to come from your assets or a part-time job. Perhaps you owner-financed the sale of your business and get paid monthly, or you have rental properties that provide you income. Your investments can be used to generate income. Your assets can fill a very important income gap for you until you are eligible for social security or a pension.

ASSETS

Assets are the key to retiring early. A person can be loaded with debt but still have enough assets to overcome their debt issue. However, if someone has a load of debt but no assets, then early retirement is most likely out of the question.

I consider assets to be such things as your home, bank account and investment account balances, 401k's, and other retirement accounts, as well as other real estate such as rental properties, life insurance cash value, and collectables. An asset is anything that holds its value and appreciates over time.

LIFESTYLE

Ask yourself: How do I live?

Do you live paycheck to paycheck, spending every dime you make just to keep up with the Joneses? Do you save 10 percent of your income each week? Do you get by with the bare necessities?

How you live your life can either be very freeing or feel like you're dragging an anchor behind you. I got sucked into that game for about ten years: buying bigger homes, newer cars, country club membership, and so on. Then, one day I woke up and thought to myself, "This isn't living." I felt like I was trapped in my lifestyle and had no freedom. The "keeping up with the Joneses" is a game you will never win unless perhaps you're Bill Gates or Warren Buffet. At my core, I'm a simple farm boy, but getting sucked into that show-off lifestyle was a real eye-opening experience for me.

The simpler your lifestyle, the easier it will be for you to

CAN YOU RETIRE EARLY IF...

...you have debt, no income, very little assets, and an extravagant lifestyle? The answer is NO. This position does not lead to a positive outcome when determining your success in retiring.

...ideally, you have no debt, good passive income, good assets, and a frugal lifestyle? The key to the four areas that make up the D.I.A.L. is your lifestyle in retirement. If you plan on an extravagant lifestyle when you retire early, then you must have the assets and income to back that up.

...you have a little debt, some income, some assets, and a very frugal lifestyle? Yes, you can still pull off a successful retirement at age fifty-five. The key is being prepared and knowing your financial numbers before you start giving your notice at work. Have a budget and have a plan.

retire early. The more extravagant your lifestyle, the more difficult it will be to retire at a younger age, unless of course you have extravagant assets to support that lifestyle.

To retire early, you must get your debt in order, have an income plan, have the assets to support your early retirement decision, and re-evaluate your lifestyle.

We'll explore each of these areas in this section.

I can assure you, when your financial plan is solid, you can retire with peace of mind knowing that you are in good shape. There's nothing worse than constantly worrying about money.

This book is all about planning for retirement so you can stop worrying about retiring and start pursuing your dreams.

So, turn the page and let's D.I.A.L. into your early retirement.

CHAPTER ONE

Debt

Advertising has us chasing cars and clothes, working jobs we hate so we can buy shit we don't need.

—Tyler Durden, *Fight Club*

Debt is like other four-letter words, which, when spoken to you, feels like a punch in the gut. Most people throughout their lifetime collect the literal meaning of debt: money owed by one party (borrower or debtor) to another party (a lender or creditor). Being in debt can add stress and worry, especially if that debt is overwhelming. However, with focus and discipline, your debt can be overcome.

Debt can be defined in three ways: good debt, bad debt, and (the best) no debt.

Good Debt

So, what's a good debt? There is no such thing as good debt. Some might argue if you're making payments on something that appreciates in value, it could be considered good debt since you're still making payments. Take, for example, your home. Most people have a mortgage payment, so you owe the bank a balance for your home. What you hope for is that while you continue to make payments your home continues to appreciate. According to Zillow.com, from April 2016– April 2017, home prices increased by 7.3 percent.

I don't consider an item that you're making payments on, such as a house, a good debt. I consider it an asset if the underlying item appreciates in value.

If you own your own business, that can be considered an asset since it can appreciate over time. A vacation home, rental homes, and raw land can all be considered assets. But if your business dries up or the real estate market takes a tumble, you go from an asset to a bad debt, so use this as a rule. We cover assets in depth in Chapter 3.

Bad Debt

If good debts are assets that appreciate in value, then bad debts are items that depreciate in value. Think of it this way, bad debts are anything you buy that either loses value as soon as you buy it or costs you something once you purchase it.

STOP BUYING STUFF YOU DON'T NEED

Another example of bad debt is just buying stuff you don't need and charging it. Whether it be clothes, a new smart phone after every new release, electronics, that new fancy coffee maker or anything else you might use a few times and not use again. Exercise equipment is something many folks are excited to buy. They use it for a month and then it sits. I have a spin bike that I had to have and now it sits in the corner as a device where I hang my clothes.

There is a lot of waste in our world, not only money waste but also stuff just lying around our homes that we don't use.

We've all heard that when you buy a new car, you lose 10–20 percent of its value when you drive it off the lot. I once had a client go buy a brand-new Dodge, drove it for a week, and decided he didn't like the car. Instead of taking it back to the dealership where he bought it and potentially working out a deal, he took it to another dealer and traded it in for a new Toyota. He lost thousands of dollars.

Credit Cards

Credit cards certainly fall into the bad debt category unless you pay them off monthly. Credit card companies are very crafty in how they pull you in with incentives: cash back, double cash back, no yearly fee, sky miles, and the good ole zero percent interest for a year. The problem lies in, culturally, we are an instant-gratification society. We see that new tech gizmo and we must have it . . . now. So, we whip out the good ole credit card and purchase it.

> ### DEBT GONE BAD
> Yes, good debt can go bad. I don't see this that often but when I do it makes me cringe. When I see a sixty-five-year-old buy or build a 3000+ sq. ft. home accompanied by a $500,000+ 30-year mortgage, I just shake my head and wonder why? Granted, sometimes there are good reasons. Perhaps they are taking care of Mom or Dad, or perhaps both and need the space. Sometimes I'll hear that they are doing it as an investment, which can work out but sometimes it may not. At the end of the day, having a large mortgage payment in retirement would be best avoided if possible.

The way to pull one over on the credit card companies is to pay off your balance each month and collect your cash bonuses and sky miles at no annual fee and no interest charge. The average interest rate on a credit card today is 16.5 percent, which means if you carry a $10,000 balance over the course of a year, you will pay $1650 in interest that year.

The more credit card debt you rack up, the bigger the mountain it is to climb to get out of it. I went through a divorce years ago and had monstrous debt due to credit cards. Plus, my interest rate on the two cards was 28 percent. It made me nauseous to even think about it. All I wanted to do was stick my head in the sand and wish it away.

One day, I just got fed up and I called the companies to see what I could work out. Expecting the worst, I was pleasantly surprised that they would work with me. If I agreed to close the accounts and not use them anymore, they agreed to drop my interest rate to 4 percent and work with me to get them paid off. It took me about three years, but I got them to a zero balance.

KNOW YOUR CREDIT SCORE

Let's talk about your credit score. According to Investopedia.com, back in 1956, an engineer named Bill Fair and his partner, mathematician Earl Isaac, developed a scoring algorithm that measured businesses and individuals' ability to pay back a loan. The company is better known today as FICO as in your FICO score. The other major credit scoring companies are Equifax, TransUnion, and Experian. Although each company has a slightly different scoring system, most have a scoring range between 300–850. The range is represented with 300 being the worst score and 850 being the best score.

Go look at the three credit agency websites (www.equifax.com, www.transunion.com, www.experian.com) and what do you see? They all sell you your score, along with a credit monitoring service, identity protection, and even which credit card companies have the best deal right now. That's like a weight loss clinic saying, "Don't forget to grab the Snickers bar on the way out." These companies determine how much we can borrow, yet they are trying to sell us on credit cards. In the financial world, there is a need to rank the risk of borrowers because companies need to know whether you can repay a loan.

You can also get your credit score for free these days as most banks and credit card companies will give you your score at no cost. Every year you are allowed a free credit report at www.annualcreditreport.com, so go online for your free credit score and report today. Getting your credit report gives you a clear picture on what negatively and positively impacts your credit score. It also allows you to view and dispute erroneous information. In the day and age of identity theft, be sure to check your report at least once a year.

A few years ago, I was in this mad dash to pay off debt. I couldn't get out of debt fast enough and I closed two of my credit card accounts. Lo and behold, I discovered that my credit score went down by closing the two cards out. Now, common sense would tell us, if you no longer have access to those credit lines and they are paid off, then your score would go up. No, I was told closing them was bad and it reduced my overall total borrowing power and lowered my average credit history. WHAT? It really makes no sense to me. My advice is to pay off your credit cards but do not close them out.

I once had a client who had $950,000 in treasury bills and another $65,000 in the bank. She went to her bank one day because she got a notice that she bounced a check. The banker suggested that she apply for overdraft protection so if she bounced another check, the line of credit would cover it. So, my client applied for the overdraft protection and she was rejected because her credit score was 350. You see my client had no mortgage, no credit card, no car payment, and no loan of any type. She was worth well over $1.5 million, but her bank would not provide her a line of credit because her credit score was too low.

If we must play by the rules the credit scoring companies give us, what is the best way to play? The best way is to have a couple of credit cards and pay them off every month and please, do not close them, even if you aren't using them. Be sure to pay on time because your credit score will be penalized heavily if you start paying your bills late.

Also, be careful of too many credit inquires. If you apply for multiple credit lines, such as buying a house, a car, applying for a new credit card and a department store card all in the same month, be prepared for your credit score to go down. Too many inquiries have a negative effect on your score. Typically, a hard inquiry into your credit by a bank or credit card company will affect your credit score for a year and drop off your credit score after two years. And if you are thinking of purchasing a house, be sure to have no inquiries on your account six months before purchasing. You can also check with your bank's mortgage department to see what you'll need to qualify for a loan.

If you have credit card debt and especially if you feel like you are in a deep hole with your credit cards, think of it as a marathon and not a sprint when paying it off. Call the company and talk with them. You might be amazed at what they can do for you.

No Debt

Having no debt whatsoever is the absolute best position. Being debt free gives you freedom and flexibility to put your income and assets to work without having to pay off or pay down bills. For years as a financial advisor and retirement specialist, I advised clients to try and have their homes, credit cards, and cars paid off prior to retiring. Some heeded my advice and some didn't. The ones who didn't found that life in retirement could still be stressful paying that large mortgage every month.

Dave and Sally came to me about five years ago with an extreme problem. They were in their late forties and were in debt well over what they could afford. They had every single debt you could imagine. Two car payments, five credit cards, a mortgage, a home equity line, two loans from a high interest lender, and they were two months behind

BANKS

If you walked into a bank today and deposited money in a CD, you might get 1 percent interest on your funds. If you came back tomorrow and needed to borrow money to buy a car, you'll probably be charged 5 percent. The bank is paying you 1 percent but charging you .5 percent. So, the bank makes a 4 percent spread on the transaction. This is how banks get paid. Not only do they make a spread off loans and deposits, but they also make money selling you other products, such as credit cards (which are huge money makers for banks), investment services, trust services, and life insurance—not to mention the fees that get charged if you drop below a certain balance, bounce a check, or want to wire money.

For years, I sat in bank meetings where they reviewed the profits for the previous month. It was stunning how much the bank made off other services. I knew from an investment service standpoint that we made the bank a lot of money. What I wasn't aware of was how much banks made off credit cards. There are two sides to this profit number. One is the fee that banks take when they install their credit card machine in a business: Banks make huge profits off credit card transactions with businesses. The second, when you're charging over 16 percent interest on a credit card, you're going to make a lot of money from that as well.

My eye-opening moment at a bank is when I learned about the 1–5 scale when it comes to ranking the best customer. The scale says that a customer with a score of 1 is a customer that is not profitable and a score of 5 is the most profitable, the best customer. So, the person with $1 million dollars in CDs and $100,000 in their checking account is a 5 on the customer scale, right? Wrong. That client would probably be a 1 on the client scale. A 5 on the customer scale is a customer who is behind on their loans and charged a late fee. They bounced 25 checks in the last year, their low balances create services charges, and their credit cards are past due accumulating late fees. These customers create the most revenue for a bank.

Most medium-size and large banks have incentive programs. An incentive program is where the customer service person, teller or branch manager is incentivized to cross-sell you another product. Banks know that if you only have a checking account with them you are at risk of leaving and moving to another bank. However, if you have a checking account, a CD, an investment account, mortgage, and a credit card, then you are anchored down and less likely to seek another bank. So, over the last 10–15 years, the push has been to cross-sell you on all the products so they can solidify the relationship; they know you're not going anywhere. The incentive programs have gotten out of hand over the years (see Wells Fargo, http://money.cnn.com/2017/08/31/investing/wells-fargo-fake-accounts/index.html, which got into trouble because bankers opened fake accounts to reach their goals).

Banks are in business to make a profit. Be sure to shop around for the best rates. You might love the bank you have done business with these past twenty years, but it benefits you to shop around and see what others are paying. You might get a better rate.

HOW TO FIND A GOOD BANK

There are many factors in choosing a bank or credit union. Ultimately, whether you are looking for a new bank or looking to make a change from your current bank, you must find a bank that matches your needs and lifestyle. If you plan to stay local, then your decision might be easy. However, if you plan to travel across the country or out of the country, then you'll want to find a bank that offers the services you'll require.

Here are nine things you should seek when looking for a good bank.

1. **Insurance**: Make sure the bank you deal with has FDIC insurance, or if you are looking at credit unions, make sure they have insurance through the National Credit Union Association.
2. **Branch locations**: Do you need the branch nearby? Are you traveling across the country and need branches located across the country? With technology these days, many people haven't been inside a bank branch in years, so you may need a physical branch location, or you may not.
3. **Online options**: Does the bank offer online services such as bill pay? Are you able to check your balances and transfer money? You certainly want to make sure these are all free services through the bank.
4. **Interest rates**: You want to make as much on your money as you can. You also want to pay the least amount if you have a loan. It pays to shop around. Banks have a deposit-loan ratio that they like to keep in line. Sometimes the ratios get out of balance and banks need deposits, so they offer a higher rate to gain more deposits, thus getting their ratio back in line. Sometimes they need loans, so they offer a special loan rate. This also helps you, so shop around and see which banks might be offering promotional rates.
5. **Minimum account balances**: Many banks have account minimums, charging you a fee if you don't stay above a certain balance. Make sure you know the minimum balance requirements or find a bank that does not have a fee.
6. **ATM fees**: Many banks rebate your ATM fees, up to a certain amount, if you use your ATM card at another bank. This is a great benefit if you use your ATM card often. If you travel a lot, make sure your bank is in an ATM network that is easy to access across the country.

7. **Mobile options**: Many banks offer an app, which allows you to check your balances, transfer money between accounts, and make deposits.
8. **Customer service**: If you have a problem, you want a bank that can take care of it quickly. Sitting on hold waiting for a representative isn't fun. When you find a great banker who you can develop a relationship with, they're worth their weight in gold. You know you have a contact person who can help you whether you're in town or out traveling.
9. **Fees**: Get a list of your current bank's fees and compare them against the other banks you are looking to potentially move to. If you plan on traveling outside the United States, how much will an international wire transfer cost? How much will it cost to exchange currency?

Also ask your friends who they deal with and what their experience has been—often their input can help you make an informed decision.

on all of them. They had good jobs, so first I had to figure out how they got into such financial deep water. It turned out Dave and Sally liked to gamble at the casino, and not just a few times a year but three times a week. They had mortgaged their future due to their addiction to gambling. They were contemplating filing for bankruptcy due to what they felt was a mountain of debt to climb over. By the time I met them, they had realized their gambling was out of control and they had not been back to a casino for three months.

I remember thinking that Dave and Sally were broken people. It was like the life had been sucked out of them because they couldn't see their way out. It was time to buckle down and get serious. I structured a plan for them to start paying off their debts one at a time. I had them come into my office every month for three years, because I wanted to hold them accountable to the plan we designed, and they wanted and needed to be held accountable. After three years, they were completely out of debt and their credit score had risen by over 200 points.

Today, Dave and Sally are happy and free. Their relationship is the best it's been in years and they haven't been back to a casino. However, they will not be able to retire early because they still have some catching up to do, but the weight of their debt is gone.

Being debt free puts you in control of your future. Think about it, when you have debt, then a company has control over you until that debt is paid off. When you don't have debt, you are the one in control.

Take Control of Debt

Being loaded down with credit card debt and car payments can be crippling. If you ask most couples "What causes the most friction in your marriage?" I bet 80 percent of the time the answer will be money, which causes stress that can fracture a relationship.

There have been times when I've had couples in my office who start to argue because they disagree about how to handle their money. A few times over my career, I've had to make up a reason to leave the room because tensions rose to such a high degree. If you have money stress as a couple, the best way to overcome it is to communicate. Playing the blame game isn't going to help matters. It takes both spouses, getting on the same financial page, to get out of that stress.

So, how do you get control of the debt versus having the debt control you? The worst thing you can do is play ostrich, like I did, and just bury your head in the sand. From a couple's standpoint, the best way to handle it is for both spouses to get on the same page about how to get rid of the debt.

I've met with over 8000 individuals and couples in my career and I've noticed a thing or two about relationships. In the financial world, couples are rarely on the same page. In almost all couples, one will be the spender and the other will be a saver. When it comes to investing, you'll have one that is more conservative and the other more aggressive. Most of the time, the saver is the more conservative investor and the spender is the more aggressive investor. This works out well because the couple will balance each other out. When you have a couple who are both savers and more conservative investors this is a perfect combination for accumulating assets. Generally, they are the ones you'll find financially ready to retire early—frugality is a very important ingredient in the retiring early recipe.

Now, if you have a couple who both are spenders and aggressive investors, it's a recipe for disaster. Typically, this couple will be riddled with debt and can make some bad investment decisions. There is no counterbalance in the relationship, which is not good. Two spenders will almost always feed off each other causing their financial situation to grow increasingly dire.

To conquer debt, look at your own situation and determine what you are. Are you a spender or a saver? Are you more conservative or more aggressive? If you are the saver, then you are the best person in the family to lead the charge to eliminate debt.

Eliminate Debt

So how do we eliminate debt? I'm sure you have heard the old saying, "How do you eat an elephant? One bite at a time." It's the same philosophy when eliminating debt.

1. Identify your debt. Make a spreadsheet or put it on a poster board and list who you owe the debt to, the total amount, the interest rate you are paying, the minimum payment, and when the bill is due.

2. Rank your debt by amount, starting with the smallest debt at the top. Your largest debt should be the last on the list.

3. Set a game plan. Start paying down the smallest debt first and keep moving down your list. Each time you pay off a debt, take the money you were paying on it and roll it to the next debt. Celebrate your successes along the way. This plan is called the snowball method.

Here is an example of how it works:

Let's say you have four different debts:	
Credit card	$1800 balance
Car payment	$7500 balance
Medical bill	$500 balance
Student loan	$9000 balance
You want to re-rank them from smallest to largest:	
Medical bill	$500
Credit card	$1800
Car payment	$7500
Student loan	$9000

First, you want to start attacking the medical bill. Let's say your minimum payment on that bill is $25 a month. However, you have an extra $200 to put on your bills so instead of spreading the $200 over all four bills, we're going to concentrate on the medical bill first. Take the $25 minimum payment and add in the $200 extra, which gives you $225 to pay down the medical bill. Within three months, you'll have that medical bill paid off.

Second, let's focus on the credit card. Your credit card has a minimum payment of $50 a month. Because you paid off the medical bill that freed up $225, which you can start adding to the credit card balance. Between the $50 minimum payment and the extra $225 you now have $275 to start paying down the balance of the credit card. Once the credit card is paid off, you now take the $275 a month along with the car payment and start paying that off. Before long you will have the car paid off and then you're able to attack the student loan.

Hence, the snowball method. Much like a small snowball rolling downhill, getting bigger and bigger as it collects more snow along

> ### RETIRE EARLY TRENDS
> Several trends we are seeing regarding housing with folks looking to retire early is that folks are selling their home and possessions and moving into RVs and roaming the countryside full-time. They are also moving to countries like Mexico, Panama, and Costa Rica where the cost of living is cheap.

the way. The snowball method for paying off debt starts with your smallest debt and, as you pay off balances, allows you to put more toward the next balances as you pay off the previous ones.

4. Once you have the debt paid off, remember don't close your cards. This can have a negative effect on your credit score. I'd suggest sticking one in your wallet or purse and leaving the others at home. I've had clients in the past that stuck the spare cards in their safety deposit box at their bank because they didn't trust themselves with the cards. Do what works best for you. If you need to hide them from yourself, then hide them.

In twenty-four years as a financial advisor, I can say I have been wowed only twice in my career by couples under age forty. Most couples under age forty come in with the same debt issues and educational issues (needing to save for college), and most aren't thinking too hard about retirement. What wowed me about the two couples? One couple came in with a spreadsheet listing all their assets. Tracking assets is always a good sign. Most folks don't come into my office that prepared. This couple were professionals, but they weren't doctors or lawyers. Since they were both thirty-six years old, I was astonished that they had saved almost a million dollars in their brokerage and retirement accounts. The second couple came in a few years later and the husband was forty and his wife was thirty-seven. Once again, the spreadsheet came out with a list of their assets. I was extremely impressed to see assets well over $1 million between mostly investments and a second home.

I see people all the time who have impressive assets, but normally not from folks under age forty. I asked both couples their secret. How were they able to succeed in saving so much during their twenties and thirties when normally that is a very expensive time for a young couple? Both gave almost the exact answer: "We are very frugal with our money. We track our expenses and make sure we are saving twenty percent or more of what we are earning. We are also very intentional in what we buy so we only buy the things we need."

The key word I got out of both conversations was the word "intentional." The definition of intentional is deliberate or done on purpose. Another way to think about it is being mindful with the way you

BE FRUGAL

Let's talk about being frugal because this really is, at its core, the one trait that will get you retired much earlier than your friends and family. Being frugal means that you are prudent and not wasteful when managing your money. As an advisor, I've met with quite a few frugal people and none of them seemed to be unhappy because they didn't have the biggest home or the newest car. On the contrary, they seemed more at peace and comfortable with their lifestyle.

Is being frugal a learned behavior or is it something we are born with? From what I have seen and learned as an advisor, my guess is both. We tend to be a product of our surroundings, so if you grew up with a Mom and Dad who were frugal, chances are their money management style rubbed off on you. But that might not always be the case because some folks rebel against their upbringing and do the exact opposite of the way they were raised. If you grew up in a family of spenders, then you potentially are going to be a spender as you grow older.

Certain personality types tend to be frugal. Think of it this way. Have you ever met an engineer or an accountant with an outrageous personality? Probably not. Most engineers and accountants are number geeks and tend to have reserved personalities. Being good with numbers and being reserved are an ideal combination to being frugal. Farmers and college professors tend to be more frugal. On the opposite side, people who are in sales tend to have more of a spender mentality. Your personality and the money management skills you were exposed to when you were growing up won't always predict whether you are going to be frugal or a spender, but they certainly can influence the way you manage your own money.

Most individuals or couples who are frugal are probably never going to want to change and suddenly become spenders. It's almost as if once you have become frugal you stay frugal. However, spenders often want to become frugal, but they just don't know how. I call this spender rehab because it's going to take some time to change your mindset. Most spenders don't have a budget, nor do they track their expenses and getting into a habit of doing so can be more difficult. However, it is very possible to make that change with a little work.

So, how do you start to convert to being more frugal? Start tracking everything you spend money on. These days it's so easy to do with apps like Mint (www.mint .com), which can track your expenses. If you don't track expenses, you will lose track of where your money is going. I've always suggested to clients that you probably know, off the top of your head, where 85 percent of your money is going each month. The other 15 percent of your funds is like a black hole where your money disappears. You can't account for it. Most of the time it's in the form of eating out at restaurants, that $5 latte you get every day, or some other overlooked activity. Until you can track where you are spending your money, you are not going to be able to correct your spending habits.

I've been on every imaginable diet there is. I've read multiple weight loss books, and been to nutritionists, Weight Watchers, and participated in almost every fad diet there is. At the end of the day, I know the formula is simple. I need to eat less calories and exercise. What does nearly every weight loss program start you off with? A food journal. You need to write down everything you eat so you can see how many calories you are eating and then you can monitor and adjust your diet. It's the same with money and the formula is simple: spend less, save more, and track your expenses.

I have met folks in the past who woke up one day and said, "I have had enough" and quit their job without much preparation. Although satisfying in the short-term, this normally does not bode well for retiring early.

As a financial advisor, I've had several clients in the past who have come in and told me they're getting ready to quit their job due to stress or burnout. My first response is generally not my professional response because it tends to be "Good for you." Then I put on my advisor hat and say, "Wait a minute, let's make sure your finances are in order before you make the jump." However pleasing it might be to tell your boss that you quit, you really want to make sure your finances are in order before doing so.

Retiring early takes a lot of thought and planning. Let's say John and Nancy are both fifty-three years old and are looking at retiring next year. Based on the social security life expectancy tables, John is expected to live to 82.5 years and Nancy is expected to live to 85.7 years. So, John has 29.5 years to plan for and Nancy has 32.7 years to plan, which means it's entirely possible that John and Sally could be in retirement longer than they worked in their career. Would it be possible for John and Nancy to retire early? It's very possible if they have paid attention to their retirement D.I.A.L.

spend your money. I have certainly been guilty in the past of not being mindful and making reckless purchases. Being organized is also a sign of someone being frugal. When folks come in to my office with a notebook that has their budget and their bank, brokerage, and retirement account statements, this is a sign of an organized and, normally, a frugal person or couple.

The people who I truly see succeed in staying out of debt and really growing their assets have some specific traits. They tend to be the savers, who are more conservative, mindful of their purchases and expenses, and disciplined to invest and save. So, if I get asked by a twenty-year-old, "What is the best advice you would give a younger person who would like to retire early?" I say: live within your means, save as much as you can, track all your expenses and savings, take advantage of inexpensive index mutual funds, fund a Roth IRA, and take advantage of your company's retirement plan.

Additional suggestion: try your best to be debt free when you retire. If you have no debt in retirement, you have great freedom and flexibility. For one thing, not having a mortgage, car payments or credit card payments, will give you more income to spend in retirement.

CONSISTENTLY LIVE BELOW YOUR MEANS

Most people live paycheck to paycheck. When you work hard, it's natural to want to enjoy that success, whether it's in the form of a nice car, a spacious home, or a string of luxury vacations year after year. But if you're truly set on retiring early, you'll need to make a habit of living well below your means, both now and in the future.

Imagine you currently bring home $5,000 a month and spend every cent. Unless you somehow accumulate enough savings to replace that income in its entirety, you're going to struggle once you stop working. That's because you'll have gotten used to a certain lifestyle, and the older we get, the harder it becomes to adjust. On the other hand, if you learn to live below your means now, you'll not only get by on much less in retirement but get pleasure out of the lifestyle that comes with it.

Action Plan

When at all possible, debt is to be avoided. If it can't be avoided, then try to pay off the debt as quickly as possible. We are in an immediate gratification society, which feeds right into folks accumulating debt.

Can you live without accumulating debt? Absolutely. It takes discipline and patience to do so. It's not fun to put off the items you really want to buy when you can't pay cash for it when you have a credit card that allows you to make the purchase today.

This book is about gaining your freedom. Going in to debt is not "freeing," rather it's an anchor that weighs you down. So here is your list of things to do:

- ✓ Reevaluate your purchasing habits and develop a plan that helps you become more mindful in the way you handle your money.
- ✓ Assess your current debt.
- ✓ Create a plan (snowball method) to eliminate your debt.
- ✓ Be very meticulous on tracking your balance payoffs.
- ✓ When you are debt free, celebrate your newfound freedom.

When there is no debt, you are much closer to gaining your freedom.

CHAPTER TWO

Income

It is better to have a permanent income than to be fascinating.

—Oscar Wilde

Without income, retiring early is not possible. We all need a way to sustain a living lifestyle and without income, we're not going to have the means to live the life we want.

If you look up "How much income will I need in retirement?" you'll generally come across a number like 70–80 percent. What this means is you'll need 70–80 percent of the income in retirement based on the salary you had when you were working. For example, if you were making $60k a year when you were working, you'll need $42–46k in retirement to sustain your current level of living. Now this is just a general rule—your own situation might be quite different as you might need more (or less) than those numbers. Keep in mind, this figure does not take inflation into consideration. Inflation is the cost of goods appreciating over time, so you might need more in ten years than you need today.

As a financial advisor, I remember sitting in New York City in my training class and hearing these same numbers back in 1994. I've continued to hear the same percentages throughout my career. This assumption has not changed at all over the years.

I do agree with the percentages if you plan on retiring at age sixty-five. However, if you're looking to retire at age fifty, a good rule would be to try and live off 50 percent of what you were making. If you plan on retiring at age forty, then try to live off 40 percent of what you were making. As I compiled the research for this book, I'm finding people who have retired early are managing to live on 80–90 percent less income from when they were working. I've spoken with many Americans who currently live in foreign countries. Recently, I struck up a conversation with a young digital nomad (someone who can work anywhere in the world and use technology to perform their job), who currently lives in Thailand. His job is 100 percent online and he makes about $10,000 a month doing so. He told me that he spends only about $800 a month for all his expenses. Plus, he said he only works about 15 hours a week.

If you want to be free, you'll find a way to make it happen.

Remember, my definition of retirement is not stopping work. My definition is to do what you want to do, when you want to do it. Leave the bullying boss, the corporate goals, the stress and sleepless nights, and the 9–5 job behind. Work on your terms.

So, let's get started on how you're going to get income if you're no longer working a career.

Pension

If you work for the Federal, State or Local Government, the military, many union jobs and some corporations, it's possible you may have a pension benefit that you can count on when you retire early. I see a sizable number of folks retiring from the military in their mid-forties with around 50–60 percent of the highest thirty-six months of base pay. Having a pension you can turn on before age fifty-five is a huge benefit. Many corporate pension plans are based on the model that if you have worked twenty years and are age fifty-five, you can turn on your pension if you leave the company. If you worked less than twenty years at the company, then you'll have to wait until you're sixty-five to turn it on.

Over the past twenty years, pensions have been dying off. The main reason is because people are living longer. In the 1960s, a male's life expectancy was around sixty-six years old and a female's was seventy-three years old. So, if you were a male and retired at age sixty-two, you had four years of life expectancy left. Four years isn't long for a company to pay out a pension. Nowadays, the average life expectancy for males and females is in the eighties. It's common for a corporation to be on the hook for twenty or even thirty years paying a pension. Many companies have run the numbers and found pensions too expensive and eliminated them.

If you have a pension, count yourself lucky.

Social Security

The Social Security Act was passed into law back in 1935 and the first check was issued in 1940 for $22.54. For many years, you had to wait until age sixty-five to collect your social security. In 1961, another law passed that enabled folks to take a reduced benefit at age sixty-two. In 1983, again, another law raised the full retirement age to sixty-six and two months for those born in 1955 or later. In the ensuing years, the retirement age will gradually increase to age sixty-seven for those born in 1960 or later. So, now, I cannot receive my full retirement benefits until I'm sixty-seven years old.

Social security has been called the world's largest annuity because, like an annuity or pension, it provides an income stream that you can't outlive. When it was first enacted, it was called social insurance because the country was still recovering from the Great Depression in the 1930s. The country needed a program to assist older folks who had very little money to take care of themselves. Much of social security is funded through payroll taxes, so, for example, in 2018, you'll pay into social security up to $128,400 of your earnings.

You have probably heard or seen that in 2034, the social security trust is due to run out of money. That isn't exactly true because the payroll taxes will continue to make up for about 75 percent of the payments needed. How did we get here? Again, because we are living longer. In 1935, the average life expectancy was age sixty-one, so a sizable portion of the population did not reach full retirement age. Today, according to the Social Security Administration, the average life expectancy is age eighty-four. Thus, increasingly more people are using social security. And we have a larger aging population—the number of folks applying for social security over the next twenty years is going to skyrocket putting stress on the program.

So, should we depend on social security? I'm of the thought that social security will not go away but the benefits may be reduced in the future. Perhaps the reduced benefit and full-benefit ages are pushed higher, so you receive your reduced benefit at sixty-eight and full benefit at seventy-two or something like that. In the end, it's better to be prepared when future changes do come to social security.

We shall discuss social security more in Chapter Six.

Annuities

Social Security, pensions, and annuities all provide lifetime income and are the only three items that can. Matter of fact, social security is deemed the largest annuity in existence.

What is an annuity?

An annuity is a contract with an insurance company that provides a payment stream for the rest of a person's life. They come in a variety of products, which we'll discuss more in Chapter Three.

Social Security is a program that you pay in to and then at age sixty-two or later, you can get a lifetime income stream. Pensions are provided by employers as an incentive and benefit for employees that stay with them for a prolonged period. Once the employee retires, depending on the terms of the pension, the employee can receive a lifetime income stream from their pension.

Annuities provide an opportunity to set up your own personal pension plan, which will provide you a lifetime income stream. Most annuities are very predictable in the income they provide whether you start income immediately or choose to defer the income and start it five years later.

Be careful. There are two types of income streams that annuities offer, and you need to know the difference between them. One annuity income stream is called a lifetime income rider. This is an income benefit (rider) that can be added on to your core annuity contract. These income streams are generally flexible—you'll be able to start the income payment, stop it, increase your payment, and decrease your payment—you are in control of your money. The second annuity income stream is called annuitization. This is when the annuity company sends you payments for a specific period or for the rest of your life. The tricky part here is that you lose control of your money. Once the payments are set up, there is no going back. I suggest you stay in control of your money and stick with the income riders when at all possible.

Disability Income

Having a disability is a bit different than choosing to retire early because many disabilities force you to retire early. For years I've heard horror stories from folks who have applied for disability for legit reasons only to be turned down four or five times before they were approved. I once had a client who was in a horrific car accident and was unable to stand due to a major back injury. He was rejected five times before his disability was finally approved. But once you are approved, your average lifetime earnings will determine the amount of social security disability income you will receive. The average social security disability check for 2017 was $1,171.

Besides social security disability income, there are individuals who are covered under private short-term and long-term disability plans that pay a percentage of income in case of a disability. Short-term disability plans generally start coverage from day one up to day thirty depending on the plan. Most plans will pay for the first six months and then convert over to a long-term disability plan. The length of long-term disability plans depends upon the policy that the individual has. Some will pay for a specific period and some will pay until age sixty-five. Both short-term and long-term disability plans are mostly employee benefits offered by employers although individuals can purchase these plans themselves as well.

Real Estate

Income-producing real estate is one of the most popular ways to fund your early retirement. Some of the best income-producing real estate properties are rental homes, duplexes, office and commercial buildings, vacation cabins and condos, self-storage units, and mobile home parks. If you plan to travel the country for an extended period, you can rent out your own home and turn it into an income-producing asset. Ideally, if you currently lease or rent out your property, it's great if your property is paid for but not completely necessary. I met a couple ten years ago who retired in their mid-fifties and owned seven different rental homes. None of the homes were paid off but after the taxes, insurance, mortgages, and paying the management company to oversee the properties, the couple was netting out about $2500 a month, which was enough to cover most of their monthly expenses.

What you are looking for is passive income. Passive income is income that comes in on a regular basis that takes very little effort. Rental properties are great passive income streams. Take self-storage units as an example, all the work is in the beginning when you're buying the land, pulling the permits, building the units, and hiring someone to oversee the leasing. After all that is done, you collect a monthly check as the units are rented.

While we are on the real estate topic, did you know you can buy real estate with your IRA? There is an IRA called a Self-Directed IRA, which, when done properly, will allow you to purchase real estate and other assets through your IRA.

My sister Lisa called me about two years ago telling me that her and my brother-in-law, Glenn, were looking to purchase an oceanfront condo in Myrtle Beach. They already live in Myrtle Beach, but this was going to be for rental purposes. She discussed

> ### SELF-DIRECTED IRA
> A Self-Directed IRA is a retirement account that is available to anyone and gives you the ability to invest not only in stocks, bonds, and mutual funds but also in real estate, businesses, tax liens, and many other types of real property. I've even heard of farmers using their Self-Directed IRAs to buy cattle. The real benefit with one of these types of retirement accounts is that you can buy and sell inside of the IRA and, if the money stays in the account, your account grows tax-deferred. Think of them as just another way to leverage your money.
>
> There is a lot of fraud that goes on with Self-Directed IRAs so be vigilant and do your homework. Also consult your CPA or accountant before setting one up. For more information, see https://www.sec.gov/investor/alerts/sdira.pdf.

the diverse ways she thought they could make this happen. I brought up the idea of taking their IRA and buying the property. I connected her with Equity Trust (https://www.trustetc.com/), a company out of Ohio that specializes in self-directed IRAs and they were able to transfer the IRA to this company and purchase the condo. The IRA had been sitting in an account, not making a tremendous amount of money, and now it's turned into an income-producing investment.

If you are interested in self-directed IRAs, be sure to locate a company that specializes in these types of IRAs. Early in my financial advising career, I learned from another advisor that one of his clients had gone to a local attorney who claimed they could help him set up a Self-Directed IRA. The transaction was set up incorrectly and the person ended up with a tax bill of over $250k. It kind of reminds me of the old saying: "If you think it's expensive to hire a professional to do the job, wait until you hire an amateur."

What about a reverse mortgage? A reverse mortgage is a loan that allows you to take cash out of the equity of your home. I got this question a few times a year from clients. First, you must be at least sixty-two years old to apply for a reverse mortgage. Second, I'm not a huge fan of reverse mortgages because the fees are high and if your children want your home when you pass away, they must buy it back. There are people who would argue with me about this because a reverse mortgage perhaps aided their Mom and Dad in retirement by giving them more income. I'm not saying they're not exceptions where people can benefit from a reverse mortgage but just read the fine print before doing one. My suggestion would be to use a reverse mortgage as your last option if you're in need of income.

Businesses

Your business might be your largest asset, and it could be your biggest income-producing benefit as well.

Several of my clients have sold their businesses over the years but kept the real estate that the business sat on. The benefit was that they got the chunk of their money for the business sale within the first five to ten years but then they got the rental income for many more years after that. Plus, it allowed the real estate to continue to appreciate over time and they were able to sell it for much more than if they would have included it in the sale of the business.

Owner financing your business is a fantastic way for you to get an income stream for five to ten years, plus you spread out your taxes on the sale. The risk here is if the new owner of your business stops making payments. So, you take the business back and sell it to someone else. Obviously, the risk is greatly diminished if you do your homework to whomever your selling it to.

Selling your business might work out well if your plan is to retire early. Most buyers of a new business, whether it's a current employee looking to buy or an outside party, are going to want the seller to stay involved for a year or two to ensure a smooth transition. This year or two of transition can benefit you, the seller, to help you prepare for your own transition into early retirement.

Think of it this way. You have owned a business for twenty years, gone to work every day and grinded it out. You sell the business on a Friday and now Monday, you are at home and fully retired. That can be a big adjustment going from 100mph to 0mph. If you have a year or two to transition, it will allow you to slowly unwind and adjust to being retired.

Investments

You've saved a bundle in your non-retirement brokerage accounts. Now how do you turn that into income? The answer is very carefully. When you're selling out your investment in a regular brokerage account, one of the areas you must pay attention to is taxes. For some folks, it might not be a problem. If you're very active buying and selling each year you're pretty much paying taxes each year as you go along. However, if you are a buy and hold investor, taxes might become a problem. Let's say you were one of the fortunate ones who loaded up on Apple stock back in the early 2000s, and you still have those shares today. When you start selling off shares to create income for yourself, it's going to be painful. The Internal Revenue Service (IRS) is going to want a piece of your gains. Please consult your CPA or accountant before doing so.

You must be selective when deciding how to take income from your brokerage account. Let's go back to Apple for a moment. Let's say you have $500k in Apple stock, $450k of which are taxable gains. However, the rest of your portfolio is littered with bad stock decisions and losses to the tune of about $450k. Your $450k in losses can offset your $450k in gains thus washing out your tax bill. Let's say you have more losses than gains. Then you can carry forward your losses on your taxes and can write off 3k in losses each year going forward until you use up the losses. This is called tax harvesting. My suggestion would be to examine your portfolio and see what the least tax-affected security to sell might be and start there.

So how much income can I draw from my brokerage account? This is a multi-part answer. Throughout time, there has been an ongoing debate in the financial services area about how much you can draw from your brokerage account and not affect your principal. In one corner, there are those who say a 3 percent withdrawal from a brokerage account won't hurt your principal. In the other corner, there are those who believe that withdrawing 4 percent is doable. So which number is correct? Both are. You see, the markets move in only two directions: up and down. The ideal percentage is based on how your account is doing. If you have just come off a very good year for your account, perhaps it's time to take some profits (income) and withdraw 4 percent or even more. If it's a bad year and your values are down, then take less out for income or a 3 percent withdrawal.

Where people get in trouble is when they start taking big withdrawals such as 7 percent or more from their brokerage account. This is flirting with disaster. If the markets fall off 20 percent or 30 percent, your 7 percent withdrawal becomes a 10 percent withdrawal rate. For example, let's say you have a $300,000 brokerage account invested in various mutual funds. You currently take a 7 percent withdrawal or $21,000 out each year. The market must do at least 7 percent (or more) for you to break even each year. However, in the second year the market drops 30 percent and your account is down 30 percent. Your account value is now $210,000, but you need to continue to take $21,000 out. At $300,000 a $21,000 withdrawal was 7 percent, but now at $210,000 a $21,000 withdrawal is a 10 percent withdrawal rate. At this point, you run a very real risk of running out of money in the future. A large withdrawal rate and a big dip in the market is hard to recover from.

Dividend paying stocks can offer you a great income stream.

I've seen some folks invest their funds in stocks that pay dividends between 3–5 percent and, in some cases, even higher. They live off their dividends and never touch their principal. You can often find stocks in the utility, energy, and real estate sectors that pay a higher than average dividend yield.

Retirement Accounts

Now, I'll be the first to say that using your retirement accounts (IRA, 401k, profit sharing plan, SEP or Simple) to fund your early retirement prior to age 59½ is not wise. If you withdraw money from your retirement accounts prior to age 59½, you'll pay a 10 percent early withdrawal penalty to the IRS along with federal and state taxes.

If you must use your retirement accounts, let me inform you on the best way to do so. There is an IRS code called 72T. In the financial industry, we call it rule 72T (www.irs.gov/retirement-plans/retirement-plans-faqs-regarding-substantially-equal-periodic-payments). Rule 72T allows you to take penalty-free withdrawals from your IRA based on a set of formulas calculated by the IRS, which is based on life expectancy. It allows for substantially equal periodic payments for five years or 59½, whichever is longer. This allows you to access your IRA prior to 59½ and avoid the 10 percent IRS penalty.

There is a catch. Once you start the 72T distribution, you can stop it within five years, but you will be subject to the 10 percent penalty back to the first dollar you took out. So, it's not wise to stop a 72T distribution once you have it going in the first five years. But like a lot of things in the financial world, there is a workaround. Let's say you are fifty-three years old and you have a large IRA, valued at $400k. Based on the income that you need, you could split the one IRA into two IRAs. You put $250k in one IRA and leave $150k in the second IRA. Now you set up the 72T distribution on the $250k IRA and you have the other $150k IRA as your cushion in case you were to need it. This would allow the $250k IRA to provide you income and avoid the 10 percent IRS penalty for early withdrawal, and it leaves the other IRA available for emergencies. Granted, you'd be penalized if you take a distribution from the $150k IRA because that one is not set up as a 72T plan. Again, I do not recommend taking money from your retirement prior to 59½, but if you must, I believe this is a great solution to avoid the tax penalty.

There is also a way to withdraw money from your 401k and avoid the 10 percent early withdrawal penalty. If you have left your employer at age 55 or after, you'll be able to withdraw money from your old 401k and avoid the 10 percent penalty. This benefits people between the ages of 55 and 59½. Not all plans allow this type of withdrawal, so check with your 401k plan administrator to see if it's an option.

Here are a few things to consider when doing this:

1. You must be at least 55 years old or older. For example, if you left your job at age 53 and at age 56 you withdraw funds from your old 401k, you'll be subject to the 10 percent early withdrawal penalty because you were not 55 or older when you left the job.

2. If you roll your 401k over to an IRA, you lose the ability to avoid the 10 percent penalty unless you use rule 72T.

3. You can leave XYZ company at age 55 and go to work with ABC company and still make the withdrawals from your old XYZ 401k plan. You don't have to be retired to make the withdrawal and avoid the 10 percent penalty. This is more flexible than a 72T plan. With 72T, you're at the mercy of the IRS formulas, which limit how much you can take out. There is no limit on how much you can take out of your 401k plan to avoid the 10 percent penalty. Keep in mind, you'll still need to pay federal and state tax on your withdrawals and those can add up quickly.

Roth IRAs

I love Roth IRAs. Simply put, I think they are the best and most flexible retirement accounts. Think about it, how many investments can you name that the IRS gives us that are tax free? Tax-free municipal bonds are one, along with college 529 plans (as long as the money is used for education). Then there is the Roth IRA. In 2018, a person under age fifty, can contribute $5500 to a Roth. If you are over fifty, you can contribute $6500. Roth's are subject to income limits so if you make too much money, you may be ineligible to contribute to a Roth. You can also convert your traditional IRA to a Roth IRA, nevertheless you will have to pay the federal and state tax on the amount you are converting, so it may or may not make sense to do a conversion. The younger you are, the more sense it makes to do a Roth conversion.

So how is a Roth going to allow me to retire early? A Roth IRA gives you the ability to remove the contributions you have made into it anytime without taxation. For example, James is forty-eight years old and has a Roth IRA valued at $180k. His Roth IRA has $100k in contributions that he put in and the remaining 80k are from earnings. James can take out his $100k worth of contributions prior to 59½ and not pay taxes on the distribution. But if he takes out the $80k worth of earnings, he'll pay a 10 percent early withdrawal penalty plus federal and state tax. James can take the $100k out and let the $80k stay in the Roth to grow until he's 59½ thus allowing the account to continue to grow. At 59½, he then can take out the balance of the account, tax-free.

Let's say you retire at age sixty and you have $150k in your Roth and $200k in your 401k. You are beyond age 59½ so you no longer need to worry about the 10 percent early withdrawal penalty. Your $200k in your 401k is completely taxable so as you withdraw money from that account, you'll have taxes owned. Withdrawals from retirement accounts, except for Roth IRAs, are taxed as ordinary income.

So, if you take $200k out of your 401k balance and put it in your checking account, you will get walloped with taxes, because you will show an extra $200k in income. You'd be better off taking out distributions over many years on that account to spread out the taxes. However, on your $150k Roth IRA, you can withdraw any amount that you'd like, and it will be tax free, as long as the Roth has been open for five years.

Here is a great Roth trick for retiring early. Let's say you're forty years old and have a traditional IRA that is worth $200,000. You can convert your traditional IRA to a Roth IRA. Keep in mind, you'll have to pay federal and state tax on this conversion, and it's best if you pay the taxes from money outside of your IRA. Your goal is to retire at age 47 so by doing this conversion at age 40, you'll be able to take out 100 percent of your contributions or $200,000 and use any way you'd like. Hopefully, your Roth has grown over the past seven years so the money you have earned over that time can stay in your Roth and continue to grow. At age 59½, you'll then be able to draw the remaining balance out tax-free.

Get a Job

Keep in mind, my definition differs from that of a traditional retirement. It doesn't mean you won't work a part-time job or even a full-time job. What I'm saying is that you're not going to let your career control your life. Think about what you have always wanted to do and see if you can find a job that syncs with that.

You can better accomplish my definition of retirement at a later age because you understand the economy and job market better—and probably have more assets to employ. In fact, that is a major reason you can even consider retiring. In your first twenty or thirty years of work and consumer life, you've almost certainly accumulated assets and developed abilities that can now be monetized or converted into cash.

Say you've learned to enjoy playing golf. Teach golf. No, you probably won't teach at the level of a golf pro, but you can teach someone how to play golf well enough to enjoy it. Or perhaps you're a good office manager. Hire yourself out as an office management consultant. Or you can grow a garden, lead people, fix household appliances, hustle up business for someone else. The internet and other marketing methods now allow you to market these skills relatively easy.

Also, at age forty or fifty you know a lot more about what you like. Fresh out of high school or college the work world is often a novel or bewildering experience. By forty or fifty you know a lot more about what the work world is and what joys and sorrows it holds for you.

Yes, there are experts in the areas I named above, but since you're merely trying to support your retirement goals, not achieve a big fortune, you can charge less, give your clients more time, enjoy the process in a more leisurely fashion, and thus get customers faster.

Over my career, I've averaged driving about 30,000 miles a year and have reached 51,000 miles in a year in the past—so I don't mind driving. I have a desire to see the United States and spend time in various areas especially the Southwest. One job that I heard about a few years ago that I always thought would be cool is a long-haul expeditor. An expeditor basically picks up a cargo shipment and delivers that shipment somewhere in the United States. Now I'm not talking about picking up the cargo in a semi-truck but cargo that would fit in a cargo van like a sprinter van (no CDL needed). It could be 500 miles away or 3000 miles away. Once you deliver that shipment, you can pick up another and deliver that to a different location and just keep going around the country. Say you deliver cargo to Key West and you want to enjoy Key West for a few days, you always have the option to stay there before you accept another delivery. A job like this checks off a few of my likes about a job: 1) I'm traveling across country and seeing different areas, 2) I'm driving, and 3) I don't have to think and can shut down my brain.

Becoming an Uber or Lyft driver is another effortless way you can make money. Or how about starting your own YouTube channel, blog or podcast? There are lots of ways to make money online these days, you'll just have to figure out how to take your passions and turn them into a money maker.

A few years ago, I met a friend at a concert who brought along one of his friend's from out of town. The friend of a friend had a fascinating story. He made six figures a year by buying up concert and sporting event tickets from around the country when they went on sale and then turned around and listed them on ticket broker sites. He did this all from the comforts of his own home. I thought to myself: "Wow, that is an awesome way to make a living!"

Most people get frustrated and overthink the process when trying to figure out what makes them happy and how they can generate income. Let's say your passion is cats and being around your cats makes you happy. Start a blog and call it something catchy like "Crazy Cat Nip" and start selling specialty catnips around the country. Film some cute little cat videos and post them online and before you know it, you have a business. You can monetize the blog using affiliate marketing plus make money on your product. How can you make money using affiliate marketing on a blog? Let's take a cooking blog for example. In one of your blog posts about baking, let's say you are bragging about your mixer. In your blog post you put a link to Amazon to where folks can click on it and buy the mixer. Amazon will pay you a commission if someone reads your blog, clicks your link to the mixer, and purchases it. There are thousands of companies that will pay you a commission for recommending their products.

Look at your passion and figure out how to monetize it. If you think hard enough and put some real effort into it, I bet you can figure out a way to make it happen. I'm a thinker, and my mind moves at about 100mph. I drive people crazy because I'm always coming up with new ways to do something and new business ideas.

So, if you aren't someone who thinks creatively, then find someone or even better, a group of people, who do. Then throw out your idea to the group and see what folks come up with. You'll be amazed how many ways you might be able to create cash flow off your passion.

Mobilize Your Current Job

You love your current job but you're not a major fan of going to the office 9 to 5. Increasingly more companies are allowing their employees to work from any location. Corporations are learning that an employee doesn't have to be sitting in their office building to get the results they need. Matter of fact, many companies are hiring people halfway around the world and they never step foot in the office.

You may say that working from home on the same job doesn't sound like early retirement. However, you might be able to negotiate the details of your job so that it becomes something you enjoy.

Let's assume you've decided that it's time for a change but you enjoy your job and would like to stay involved if you could. (On your terms!) Now you probably want to have a plan B before doing this because you never know what the answer might be. In an ideal world, you'd like to stay at your job, work remotely, drop your hours to twenty-five a week and still get benefits. Go offer that up to your boss and see what they say. Heck, you're out the door anyway because you've already made up your mind to leave. The worst that can happen is they say no. However, if you are a valuable employee, they very well may say yes.

So, does that mean you have to only work from home? No. Now you can be the person who is working from halfway around the world. You are now unanchored and able to live anywhere you want to live.

Action Plan

Retiring early will require you to have income, preferably multiple income streams. This requires you to do some planning in the years prior to retiring. Some people are more comfortable with real estate and others with the stock market. With the younger generations, they might ignore both real estate and stock market and develop a phone app or generate income by affiliate marketing. Play to your strengths and what area you are most comfortable with.

In the digital age we are in today, they are more ways than ever to set up an online business. You'll not just offer a product or service to your neighbor or to someone in the next state but to people all over the world. Being a digital nomad isn't just for the twenty-two-year-old anymore. Plenty of folks in their forties and fifties (me included) are learning how to navigate this digital society and make money off it.

Ask yourself:

✓ What are my current income streams? Make a list.
✓ What type of income streams do I have? Are they lifetime income streams, such as a pension, or can my income fluctuate?
✓ Are there ways I can create more income? That large certificate of deposit in the bank might be nice but it's not paying much. Can I buy a rental property and start making more income?
✓ Have I maximized all the ways I can to increase my income?
✓ Make an assessment. Will I have enough income to more than cover my lifestyle?

Generating income must come before you achieve your freedom. Once you have your income streams set up, then you are off and running.

CHAPTER THREE

Assets

Freedom is something that dies unless it's used.

—Hunter S. Thompson

I n planning to retire early, your assets play a very important role in your financial picture.

What do you own that is worth value? For most people, they will count their home, bank accounts, brokerage, annuities, and retirement accounts. Other assets could be a collection such as art, coins, classic cars, and stamps. When you total up all your assets, think of anything that has value to it. Look around, that piece of property that you own, those horses in the barn. Or if you are a business owner, your business is certainly an asset.

Why are assets important? There are many reasons why assets are important. The key reason is that they can be turned into income. Having assets gives us comfort, but it also gives us a pathway to freedom. Without assets, retiring early is very difficult because most people need assets to convert into income. You can retire early on very little assets but the more assets you have, the more freedom they will provide you.

Are you bankable? When you apply for a mortgage, the mortgage lender is going to ask for your assets and your liabilities. What they are looking for is your total net worth, which is your assets minus your liabilities. The essential point is that they are looking for your ability to repay the loan. So, having assets is important for most financial areas of your life, they prove your bankability.

Having assets also gives you more options when it comes to planning your early retirement. Do you buy that used fifteen-year-old RV in decent shape because you have limited assets, or do you buy that new loaded RV because you have the assets to afford it?

Assets can give peace of mind. The more assets you have, the less worry and second-guessing you'll do when you retire early. You have a plan in place and when you don't have to worry about money and can just follow your plan, life is less stressful.

Once you get into retirement, your plans may take a drastic left turn. Instead of downsizing your home and living locally, you decide to move to Montana. Having assets allows you the flexibility to make turns in retirement.

Assets allow room for the unexpected. "And they lived happily ever after" is how most fairy tales end. However, in our lives, we are often faced with unexpected health problems, mechanical problems, divorce, and tragedies. Having

EMERGENCY FUND

In my opinion, the most critical area of financial planning is the Emergency Fund. I don't care if you are twenty years old or a hundred years old, everyone should have an emergency fund or cushion. There are just too many things that can go wrong these days to be stuck without an emergency fund. "But, Eric, I can use my credit card as my emergency fund." No, no, no...I want to get you away from creating debt for your cushion.

How much should you have in an emergency fund? Over time, I've always heard and read that three to six months of your earnings should be saved in an emergency fund. From my experience, some folks like to have at least $10k in the bank for their cushion. For others it's more like $25k up to $100k. Now, having a $100k emergency fund sitting in the bank earning very little might be a bit much. My answer to how much you should have in an emergency fund really comes down to: How much do you need in a readily accessible bank account to sleep well at night? The answer is really a personal one for you.

assets allows us to navigate these waters more smoothly knowing that we have money to overcome many of those issues.

Your Primary Home

What is the value of your home? Do you have a mortgage on your home? If so, what is the remaining balance of your mortgage?

Let's say that your early retirement involves you taking off several years and traveling the country in an RV. Or perhaps you want to move to Mexico for a few years. Many folks find that they will keep their primary home because they may plan to move back in a few years, or they just feel more comfortable having a place to retreat to in case their plans don't work out. If you know you'll be gone for only a few years, you can always rent your home while you are out of town.

Renting your home can be a great income source especially if your home is paid off. Even if it isn't paid off, get someone to rent it so they can make the mortgage payment for you.

I live in Asheville, NC, which currently has a very hot real estate market. People are moving from all over the country to live in Asheville. My plan is to keep my home until my children get out of college and then rent it out. I'll keep the home long term but allow someone else to make the payment for me. Think of it like addition by subtraction. Subtracting your mortgage payment adds to your flexibility. Not having a mortgage payment each month because the rent I collect is paying my mortgage payment will allow me to have more flexibility with the income I bring in.

Airbnb (www.airbnb.com) is another great option for renting your home out for a week or weekend especially if you're in an area that draws a lot of tourists. VRBO (Vacation Rental by Owner, www.vrbo.com) is another option you can use to rent out your home. Stop thinking of your home as just your primary residence and think of ways to utilize this asset to retire early.

Bank Accounts

Bank accounts consist of your checking, savings, money market, and certificates of deposit (CDs). Your checking account is great for what I call your "working capital." This is where your paycheck comes in and your bill payments go out. It's not a great idea leaving a lot of money in your checking account because banks don't pay much interest these days. Your savings and money market accounts are a suitable place to leave your emergency fund or money set aside for those near-term projects like putting a new roof on your home. Here, the rate of return is not important, because it's the access to those funds which is key. Most one-year CDs average around 1 percent in interest today. At 1 percent, it will take you seventy-two years to double your money. That's right, *seventy-two* years.

So, if CDs are averaging 1 percent today and you have $50k invested in one, you'll receive $500 each year in interest. This is not a great income producer. CDs are great for safety but at the end of the day, when you factor in taxes and inflation, you're going nowhere fast.

Brokerage Accounts

You've saved and invested in stocks, bonds, mutual funds, and ETFs (Exchange Traded Funds) over the years and now it's time for those funds to start paying you back. Whether you retire at fifty or retire at sixty-five, there are two stages in investing. The first is the accumulation stage. The accumulation stage is the phase in which you are still working and investing your money. This could be in a non-retirement brokerage account or in a retirement account such as your IRA or 401k. So, you are accumulating assets over time until you retire. The second stage is the distribution stage. In this phase, you have retired and now you need your investments to provide you with an income.

Again, retiring early doesn't mean you're not going to work anymore. In effect, you could be in the accumulation stage even after you've left your career. It's entirely possible for you to continue to earn money after you leave your career and continue to accumulate assets.

Annuities

Annuities, pensions, and social security are the only three income streams that have a guaranteed lifetime income. This means that you cannot outlive your income. Annuities can be expensive and aggressively sold by advisors, yet they can also provide a lifetime income and benefits to your beneficiaries that no other investment type can provide.

> **FUN FACT**
>
> Have you ever heard of the Rule of 72? If you are trying to figure out how long it will take you to double your money, take the interest rate and divide it into 72, which tells you how many years it will take to double your money. For example, you are earning 3 percent on your money: 72 divided by 3 is 24. So, at 3 percent, it will take you twenty-four years to double your money. You can reverse it and find out what you need to make to double your money over a specific period. What would you have to make each year to double your money in 10 years? 72 divided by 10 is 7.2. So, you'll need to make 7.2 percent each year on your money to double it in ten years.

In the annuity world, there are fixed annuities, immediate annuities, fixed index annuities, and variable annuities. Just the word "annuity" conjures up all sorts of opinions, many of them negative. Oftentimes, I hear "they are too expensive" or "I have just heard so many negative things about annuities. So, I don't like them." Many also argue that they tie up your money for too long.

I'm certainly not the one to lead the annuity charge, but there is a place for them. I've had people come into my office and we discussed their goals and their desired outcome for their retirement. They mention their concerns of outliving their money and ask about ways of how they can get a guaranteed income stream. When I mention the word annuity, I hear, "Oh no, I don't like annuities." I press them and ask why, and you know what? They can't tell me. They have just heard annuities are bad.

There are large money managers who build marketing campaigns that bash annuities to try and change the public's opinion of them.

What is their reason to do so? So, they can sell you their investment portfolios. It's the classic marketing game of putting down one product to prove that their product is better. In this case, it's comparing apples to oranges. Those large money managers might have lower fees, but they can't offer lifetime income guarantees.

So, are all annuities bad? No.

Are they expensive? Not all of them. Fixed, Immediate, and Fixed Index are reasonably priced. Variable annuities can be expensive.

Should you buy an annuity? Annuities are not for everyone. Depending on your situation, they may or may not be right for you.

As an advisor for twenty-four years, I have a problem with how annuities are sold to the public. I have known and heard of advisors that 99 percent of their business was selling annuities. You can't tell me that everyone who these advisors meet with is an annuity buyer. So why do some advisors sell only annuities? The commissions are higher is probably the biggest reason. Now, is it the highest commission in the investment world? No, I have seen life insurance commissions that are higher. Plus, there are other types of investments that pay just as much commission. Just like any other investment product, such as mutual funds, stocks, and bonds, there are good ones and there are bad ones. It's the same in the annuity world.

In an ideal world, if you own an annuity, the longer you wait to start taking your income, the more income you'll receive. So, if you have an annuity at fifty-five, it would benefit you not to take any withdrawals from it until at least 59½. Waiting until sixty-five is probably even better. Be aware, if you invest in an annuity and you take a withdrawal from that annuity prior to 59½, the earnings on your annuity are taxed at your federal and state tax bracket *plus* you have a 10 percent early withdrawal penalty because you didn't wait until 59½.

I would not recommend it however. Even with an annuity, there is a way to withdraw money and avoid the 10 percent early withdrawal penalty. Remember we discussed rule 72T for accessing money from your IRA prior to 59½? An annuity has a rule called 72Q (www.gpo.gov/fdsys/

pkg/USCODE-2011-title26/pdf/USCODE-2011-title26-subtitleA-chap1-subchapB-partII-sec72.pdf), which works very similar to 72T. It allows you to take a systematic income from your non-retirement annuity and avoid paying the 10 percent penalty. Please consult a tax professional before setting up this type of plan.

Here are some of the exceptions to the above guidelines: Let's say you inherited a considerable sum of money, won the lottery or received a large settlement. An annuity, called an immediate annuity, would be a product you'd want to look at for a portion of your money, because it would give you a lifetime income and avoid the 10 percent IRS penalty at any age. BE CAREFUL! You wouldn't want to invest all your money in an immediate annuity because once you put the money in an immediate annuity, you can't get your money back unless you sell it on the secondary market where you'll take big losses.

Is an annuity right for you? Maybe or maybe not. My advice on annuities is to do your homework and make sure it fits your goals.

Retirement Accounts

Remember the candy Now and Laters? They were the taffylike candy probably responsible for pulling out a few of my teeth when I was a child. Think of your assets as Now and Laters. Your bank accounts (checking, savings, money market, and CDs) and your non-retirement brokerage accounts are your NOW money. These are the funds that, when retiring early, are the most easily accessible funds to use to retire on. Accounts such as checking, savings, money markets, and CDs are easy to access and readily available for you to use whenever you need to without a big tax bill. Ideally, your retirement accounts (IRAs, 401ks, 403Bs, SEPs and SIMPLE IRAs, and Roth IRAs) are your LATER money. We've discussed how to access your retirement accounts if you need to, however, you'd be better served holding off on withdrawing from these accounts whenever possible. It's also important to calculate the income you'll be able to generate from your retirement accounts at 59½ so you'll know what can be expected in the future. Retiring early is about having a plan and sticking to it. You want to plan on what monies will get you through from now until 59½ and then from 59½ until social security. Your retiring early plan shouldn't just take into consideration the next few years; it should consider the next forty years.

If you're a couple and both of you are fifty-two years old, keep in mind that it's entirely possible that you're going to live in retirement as long or longer than you worked in your career. So, you must prepare for today and tomorrow but also ten, twenty, and thirty years in the future.

Although there is a way to access your funds from your IRAs (see the last chapter), I highly suggest funding your early retirement from other sources. Think of your non-retirements accounts, rental income, your pay from working along the way as the means to get you to 59½. Let your retirement accounts continue to grow such that at age 59½, the retirement accounts can provide you with enough income, along with social security and possibly a pension, to get you through that next phase of life.

COMPOUND INTEREST

Investopedia defines compound interest as "Interest calculated on the initial principal and also on the accumulated interest of previous periods of a deposit or loan." Albert Einstein once was quoted as saying, "Compound interest is the eighth wonder of the world. He who understands it, earns it...he who doesn't...pays it." Warren Buffet told *Fortune* in 2010, while reiterating his philanthropic pledge, that "My wealth has come from a combination of living in America, some lucky genes, and compound interest."**

So, there must be something to this compound interest if geniuses are talking about it, right? There certainly is and it's been making people money for centuries. When thinking about compound interest, it really comes into play in two categories: saving/investing and loans. With savings and investing, you earn interest on your principal and then interest on your accumulated interest. So, for example, you invest $1000 at a 3 percent interest rate. At the end of the year, you have $1030.42 with compound interest. You earned an extra 42 cents on top of the $30 you earned in

* In 2006, Warren Buffet pledged to give most of his wealth to philanthropy. http://archive.fortune.com/2010/06/15/news/newsmakers/Warren_Buffett_Pledge_Letter.fortune/index.htm

interest. Now that doesn't sound like much, but the magic is in the length of time you leave your money to compound. Certainly, if you continue to add to your accounts each year and let them grow over a twenty- to thirty-year period, you'll be astonished on how quickly your assets add up. Over a twenty-year period, your thousand dollars would grow to $1806 and over a thirty-year period, it would be $2427 at a 3 percent interest rate. Since the length of time is extremely important when talking about compound interest, the younger you start saving/investing the more benefit it will be to you.

So, you want to be a millionaire? It's 1985, you are twenty-two years old and have $5000 saved and decide to invest your money in an S&P 500 mutual fund. You decide to add another $500 a month for the next thirty-two years. Today your value would be $1.1 million dollars after reinvesting dividends and capital gains. Now you would have paid some taxes on your account over time, but let's say that you paid those each year out of other money. Your total investment was $5000 to start and $500 a month for 32 years, which adds up to $197,000. Your $197,000 grew to $1.1 million due to the interest you earned and the compounding effect as your interest earned more interest. You'd be fifty-four years, with $1.1 million available to retire early on.

A Roth IRA is an even better investment vehicle when it comes to long-term compounding. With the above example, when you cash in the $1.1 million, there will be some tax consequences. Whereas with a Roth IRA, if you keep it to 59½ years old, you'll be able to get all your money out completely tax-free. So, in a way, it's like triple compound interest because you are earning interest on your principal, interest on your interest, and interest on the money that might be paid out due to taxes.

If you own a business, hire your children as employees and set them up a Roth IRA, you'll be stunned at how much money the account can accumulate for them over the years. For example, your daughter is fifteen years old and you hire her to do some cleaning and filing at the office. You set her up a Roth IRA and for the next three years, you deposit $3000 a year into her Roth IRA. Then you stop and never add another dime to it again. When she turns sixty years old, at an average rate of 7 percent, your daughter would have a Roth balance of $154,298 and, oh by the way, it's completely tax free. The earlier you start, the better off you'll be.

On loans, your interest will either be simple interest or compound interest. Simple interest is based on just the principle amount of the loan. Compound interest is based on the principle amount as well as the accumulated interest. Most loans are based on compound interest. So, when saving and investing, compound interest is a huge benefit. When borrowing money, compound interest isn't a benefit to you. Have your own figure to look at? Visit http://www.moneychimp.com/calculator/compound_interest_calculator.htm for a compound interest calculator to run your own numbers.

Collectibles and Other Assets

As you take inventory of your assets, you may find you have very little savings for retirement, but you just can't take working at your corporate job one more day. You spend your day staring out the window wishing you were on a Mexican beach, drinking margaritas all day. Then it hits you, you have a Mickey Mantle Rookie Card and a #1 Action Comics comic book, which by the way was the first appearance of Superman. Both are in nearly mint shape. So, here's your chance to retire because a Mickey Mantle rookie card, in nearly mint condition, sold recently for $1.1 million at auction. A #1 Action Comics, in nearly mint condition, sold for over $3.2 million at auction a few years ago. If it has value, it can be sold to fund your early retirement.

How about that vintage record collection, concert posters, coin collection? Or heck, even some of the rare Beanie Babies from the nineties are worth thousands. If it has value, it can be used to fund your retirement. (I keep repeating it because it's true.)

Granted, collectables tend to come with a lot of sentimental value because they could have been passed down through your family or a collection you've had since you were a kid. You'll have to weigh out your sentimental value versus your freedom.

I've known a few classic car collectors over the years. I'm astonished on how much some of their cars are worth. Besides watching college football, I rarely watch TV, but when I do I always enjoy watching the Barrett Jackson car auctions. It's common to see cars sell for a half million to well over a million dollars. I have known local folks that had collections worth over a million dollars.

As a collector of anything of value, keep in mind, it could possibly fund your retirement. Now, not everyone is going to have a classic car that is worth hundreds of thousands of dollars but anything of value can be sold to help you.

Business Owners

Most corporate bosses aren't going to be too understanding of your desire to retire early especially when they have revenue goals and numbers to hit. So, owning your own business can be a great resource when you are looking to fund your early retirement.

You may have a co-worker or family member run the business while you're testing out early retirement. That would be a safety net just in case you decide retiring early isn't for you. This way, you can transition back into the business if you want to in the future, or you can sell the business later.

Depending on your business, it's possible that you might be able to hire a manager and run the business from the road or even a different country. These days, as long as you have cell service, Internet access, a laptop and a printer/scanner, you can do almost anything remotely. Can your current business be mobilized?

The business that you own can provide you so many different benefits when looking at retiring early. It can be an income producer for you. It is an asset for you to sell. By selling it, you can eliminate your debt.

Life Insurance

There are two types of life insurance policies: permanent and term insurance. Permanent insurance is the type of insurance that retains a cash value. These policies are called whole life or universal life policies. As you pay your premium each year, a portion of the premium goes to pay for the life insurance and the other portion is either put in a fixed interest account or invested in the stock market. As the years pass, the insurance cost gets cheaper, which means more of your money goes into the investment side of the policy.

It's common for permanent life insurance policies to grow to a substantial amount over a twenty- to thirty-year period. So how do these make a good retiring early tool? Let's say that you have $75,000 of cash value in your life insurance policy and you cash the policy in, taking the $75,000 out of the policy. You'll be subject to taxes on the earnings that you've made over the years. However, you can take a loan out against the cash value of your life insurance policy, which is tax-free. You're able to pay off the loan in the future.

The most obvious benefit to life insurance is the death benefit paid to your family when you die. The other benefit is the loan provision. I've known people in the past who took out a loan against their whole life policy and bought stocks when the stock market experienced a 30 percent drop. As the market recovered, they sold the stocks for a nice profit and then paid back the loan on their policy. So, life insurance can give you flexibility.

I've run into quite a few folks who have forgotten they have life insurance that has a cash value on it. Many times, they just make the premium payments and forget about the purpose of the policy. When this happens, we try to evaluate whether they still need the life insurance, do they still need as much, or would it be better served into a long-term care policy. (See Chapter Five for more on long-term care.) So, be sure to re-evaluate your life insurance policy—you should know how much it is worth and what its main purpose is.

Term insurance does not have any cash value, so there is no benefit from a loan standpoint on term life insurance. With term life insurance, you strictly pay for the cost of life insurance. Term insurance is cheaper to buy, which is why a lot of people turn to it. The downside to term insurance is that it's not a lifetime policy so you must renew it when your term is up or it ends. For example, if you buy a twenty-year-term policy, in twenty years you may have a choice to convert your term policy to a permanent life policy or you can shop around for another term policy. Either way, you will pay more for your insurance because you are twenty years older than when you first got your policy.

So, is life insurance an asset? Sure. If you have a permanent life insurance policy, then you are building cash value. If you have a term policy, then it's an asset to your family when you pass away.

I'm not one of those advisors who believes everyone should buy life insurance. There are specific reasons to buy life insurance, such as having a young family, estate planning purposes, having a large mortgage, if you're a business owner, etc. There are people who just don't need it as well. Take someone older, who isn't married and doesn't have children. In this case, there is no real need to have life insurance.

Here's another way to look at life insurance. I plan on spending every dollar I have before I die. But I want to leave Kate and Frank, my two kids, an inheritance. So, I purchased a life insurance policy that will leave them a sum of money that will be their inheritance. Because death benefits on life insurance policies are paid out tax-free, they will not be burdened with taxes. What this allows me to do is spend all my money and know that my children will receive something when I die.

Action Plan

Having assets serves multiple purposes when planning on retiring early. First, you're going to need an emergency fund and your assets in the bank will cover this part. Second, you can turn your assets into income, which solves two parts of your D.I.A.L. Third, if you retire at age fifty and live until you're ninety, you'll need assets to carry you through the next forty years of your life. So, plan for today, plan for the unexpected, and plan for twenty or more years from now.

- ✓ Start building your emergency fund.
- ✓ Think: How can my assets generate income? List the ways in which you are most comfortable.
- ✓ If you have a life insurance policy, re-evaluate its purpose.

CHAPTER FOUR

Lifestyle

Freedom lies in being bold.

—Robert Frost

O ver my career, I've seen many retirement plans in peril due to a couple's lifestyle. Many couples live on the edge in retirement because of the financial choices they make. People do not generally retire early by being extravagant. Normally, the exact opposite is the case. If I had to point to one attribute a couple needs to successfully pull off early retirement, it would be being frugal.

I could kick myself for all the years that I wasn't frugal. All the wasted money on cars, houses, and stuff that I really didn't need and, in the end, none of it made me happy. We can become slaves to our possessions, then we must work jobs that sometimes we enjoy and sometimes we hate to pay for those possessions.

We can measure your (D)ebt, (I)ncome, (A)ssets by totaling them and coming up with what you owe and what you own. So how do we measure (L)ifestyle? Should we measure lifestyle by your budget? A budget is going to measure how much you are spending each month. As we discussed earlier, using an app like Mint can help you track your bills and expenses. I've met some people who would rather go to the doctor and have a colonoscopy than make a budget for one month. How do you know where you are going if you don't know where you are?

As we discussed earlier, you're either a saver or a spender. Being a saver, your default is almost automatically set to being frugal. However, if you're a spender, you might wonder how to become more of a saver to start the process of being frugal.

Try a More Minimal or Essential Lifestyle

A suggestion would be to start exploring the ideas behind minimalism and essentialism.

The principles behind both lifestyles is to free yourself from your possessions and give you more freedom in life. It's the less is more idea. Think of it this way, if you only buy the items you really need, then you not only free yourself from your stuff anchoring you down, but you also save a good bit of money in the process. I'm trying to change my own mindset by looking at an item before I buy it and asking myself, "Is this a necessity or something I just want?" I still buy stuff that isn't a necessity, but by asking myself that one little question, it helps me make a more mindful decision. For example, instead of buying eight different college football season preview magazines a year, I now only buy one.

Let's say that your home caught fire in the basement and you had five minutes to get your most prized possessions. What would those possessions be? Most likely, it would be those possessions that have sentimental value to you: photo albums, your daughter's baby blanket, the jewelry your grandmother gave you, or those love letters your spouse wrote to you. Focus on what those items are for you and think about all the other stuff that you would no longer have. Would you build back the same house and buy the same stuff to put in it or would you choose

Minimalism is defined with living with less or simplifying your life to give you more freedom.

to live life differently? You have your most prized possessions, but is the rest of your stuff just clutter?

Essentialism is living with only the essential items you need in life.

You can have some debt and still retire early. You can have very little income but still find work while you travel and make ends meet while retiring early. You can have very little assets but, as long as you are making an income, you could still retire early. But if you are living an extravagant lifestyle, you must have extravagant assets and income. If you don't have that you'll never be able to retire early and may not be able to retire at sixty-five.

You Can't Take It with You

Life is short, and I've always said, "There is no benefit in being the richest person in the graveyard." With that said, we all must prepare financially like we're living to age 100. The problem with our population is that most people's retirement plan will fail them at age ninety or before, because they have not factored in living that long. "If I would have known that I would live this long, I would have done things differently." I've heard this numerous times in my career. Don't wait until you're ninety to wish you had done it differently. Start doing it differently today.

At the end of my life, I'd rather be rich with memories filled with love and adventure than be rich with money. I've never seen a hearse pulling a safe down the road.

Freedom equals sacrifice. Unless you're wealthy, lifestyle is going to be the area that you sacrifice the most when retiring early. Many people are used to making a certain amount of money each year and our lifestyle tends to adjust to that amount of money. Generally, the more you make, the more you spend. When retiring early, very few people are going to be able to maintain their standard of living like they did when they were working.

Let's examine two different couples. Couple A are both thirty-five years old, work full-time, and bring home a combined income of $125,000 a year. Couple B are also thirty-five years old and make a combined $125k a year. Couple A live frugally and their monthly bills total around $1500 a month. They have saved about 50 percent of their income for years through investing and contributing to their 401k. Couple B are both spenders and their monthly bills are $3800 a month and they save less than 5 percent of their income. Couple A are well on their way to early retirement, perhaps even in their late thirties or early forties. (Yes, that is very possible.) Couple B are well on their way to working until age sixty-five or beyond unless they make significant changes.

I'm forty-eight years old and I have a goal to retire very soon. I'll still be working, but I'll be working from my RV or in a foreign country, on my terms. People look at me like I'm crazy when I tell them I'll be taking off in my RV for a few years and then living out my days in Mexico, Thailand, or some other less expensive country. "But you are too young to retire" is what I hear. Normally you hear this type of chatter from folks who are stuck in the retiring-at-sixty-five-year-old mindset.

You Must Sacrifice for Freedom

Are you working for money or are you working for freedom? When you work for money, you tend to focus on acquiring as much money as you can, and it seems that you will never have enough. It's been my experience that when your sole focus is money you're probably working long hours, which creates a void in other parts of your life. Often, your plan might be to work hard now so you can have the freedom later and that can work but it can backfire as well.

I have come across countless folks who became so addicted to chasing money, that even when they had enough to retire, they kept chasing. When money is your number one focus, you miss out on some key areas in your life. I never let business get in the way of my children. If there was a school play scheduled on Tuesday at 11am but a great prospective client wanted to come in at the same time, the prospective client was going to have to reschedule for another time.

My children always came first. That's not the case with everyone. I've worked with people in my career who missed their children's plays, doctor appointments, and teacher conferences because they wanted to play golf with a good prospect.

If 100 percent of your focus is on your career and chasing the all mighty dollar, you are sacrificing a lot in your life. You are putting your family second and probably your health as well. You get one chance at life, why is it so important for some to have a title behind their names and work themselves into the ground and not important for others?

The main benefit of working and chasing money is often that you achieve a level of financial success that you can ride for the rest of your life. When you retire, you can most likely strike off your list that money as a worry for you. But what did you sacrifice getting to that point? Did you take family vacations or pass on them because you were too busy? Were you not around much as a parent? Do you have regrets on how you balanced work and home? The workaholic will often find themselves divorced because the focus on their job is more important than their home life.

Freedom is the ability to do what you want to do, when you want to do it. I find most folks have a splendid work life and home life balance. Many parents are extremely active at work as well as in their children's lives. Many people find the right balance in making money and taking time off to enjoy themselves along the way.

What are we looking for when we retire? Freedom.

Why do we crave weekends? Freedom.

Why do we all want to hit the lottery? Freedom.

The air that we breathe is free. Freedom is not free because we either work to get it or buy the winning lottery ticket. So, when we decide to do something "crazy" and retire early, all we are doing is gaining our freedom. However, by retiring at fifty-five years old or younger, we must sacrifice some things to gain our freedom. By working to age sixty-five, we may be more financially stable, but we've just missed out on ten good years of freedom. Retiring early may have you cutting back financially as well as trimming back your lifestyle.

In an ideal world, you can retire at age fifty and not sacrifice anything and live your life like you've always lived it. But gaining your freedom early is going to come at a cost. You may have to downsize your home or relocate to a less expensive area. Instead of buying some new car every three years you might need to drive yours much longer.

Is Your Lifestyle Healthy?

Many of us are also sacrificing our health by not having enough freedom in our life. We get stressed and we eat junk, gain unhealthy weight and it starts affecting our overall health. I'm certainly guilty of this as my weight has bounced up and down over the years. I bet if you could track my stress level throughout the years, it would directly correlate with my weight gain. When I am mindful of this, I can get my weight down, but all too often I'm so busy with my job that I lose track. I then find every excuse in the book not to go to the gym because generally, "I'm too busy." We are all guilty of not finding the time to take care of ourselves and thus we sacrifice our health in return.

Society Pressures

In our society, there are pressures for us to act and conduct ourselves in certain ways. We are expected to go to college, settle down with that special someone and have children, work a career, and retire around the age of sixty-five. If someone bucks this trend we normally look at that person and say, "What is wrong with them?"

Deb and I have been dating for over eight years and we refer to each other as our life partner. We have no plans on getting married and we're both on the same page with it. We've had people ask us when we are getting married and Deb will normally answer them before I can: "We're not getting married. I am committed to him as much if not more than if we were married." We get a lot of questions about our not marrying from our older clients because in their minds, if you're committed to each other, you should be married. The younger generation rarely asks such questions. I've been married before and I can assure you, having a piece of paper saying you are married does not mean both parties are committed to each other.

Retiring early is not what society expects. When you tell Mom and Dad that you're moving your family and their grandchildren to Panama, don't expect a warm reception. It might be easier if you've always been the nomadic kid because they have learned to expect the unexpected from you. However, if you've always been the corporate employee with dreams of being the CEO one day, and suddenly you make a left turn into a nomadic lifestyle, be prepared for an onslaught of questions.

I have heard of couples in their late fifties taking off in their RVs and traveling North America. When they sat their children down and explained what they were going to do, they found that their children were angry with them. Some of the couples actually canceled their plans to make their children happy. Don't let your dreams be ruined by someone else who doesn't understand what makes you happy. The children will get over it and once they do, they'll probably want to join you along the way of your adventure.

I spoke to a couple about ten years ago who had the desire to retire in their late fifties. They were avid Harley Davidson riders and they wanted to make their way across the country visiting national monuments and national parks. The one thing standing in their way was their kids. I couldn't believe what the parents told me what was coming out of their children's mouths. Such as "Who is going to babysit my kids?" or the "What happens if I were to need you?" (which is code for: "What if I need money?") Then it turned into guilt: "You'll miss little Johnny taking his first step."

As parents, we must accept our role and find the balance and compromise when our plans create a problem within the family.

Comfort Zone

When you look at doing something radically different and outside of your comfort zone, keep in mind, it's going to look radically different and outside of everyone else's comfort zone as well. That is why you want to be prepared when you quit your job, sell your home, and take off. People will be jealous and wonder: "Why can't I retire at fifty?"

I've always been fascinated by the folks who live life differently like the nomads, the hippies, the guys and girls in dreads, etc. It's almost like they have their own set of rules and throw up their middle finger to what society has to say about them. There is this kid who comes to the pub that we go to who I find fascinating. He's probably in his late twenties or early thirties and has his own style, which I'd consider a nomadic style. He's traveled around the United States, jumping trains and living life. He has stories about other kids who lost their lives from being sucked under trains. Some of the folks along his way were dangerous whereas others became lifelong friends. He's fascinating because he has not lived life like we are conditioned to live our life—but boy has he lived life! He has a lifetime of stories in a brief period. Plus, he is much more interesting than sitting around the pub listening to some hipster talk about his mustache wax.

Work, Work, Work

How many people can truly say they are happy with their job? Count yourself as fortunate if you can. Most people's Monday through Friday are the same. You wake up, you have the same morning routine every morning, you drive the same route to work, you park and take a deep breath before you walk into your office building. The tasks might be different during the day but the days blend together and before you know it, Friday has arrived. You leave the office at five pm and now you have roughly sixty-two hours to unwind before returning to the same routine on Monday morning. Most of us are working for the weekends.

Look around your office and watch the zombies walk by. By zombies

I mean your co-workers who are physically there but not mentally. We live in such a distracting world with the onslaught of social media, emails, texts, and phone calls. Factor in spouses, life partners, children, parents, and it's hard to be present and mindful every day. The fact is, in our society today, we all seem overwhelmed and stressed.

Remember when our parents would go to work at a company, stay there for forty years, and walk out with a pension and a gold watch. That is extremely rare these days. Corporate loyalty seems to have diminished over the years. I've spoken to people who were fired months before they were due to be vested in their pension. I've seen bankers fired and told their jobs were being eliminated only to find that same job reposted, with the same title, a month later. I've seen employers not give their employees a raise for years, yet the company continued to buy out their competitors and spend money on other ventures. We work and work, sacrificing our health and our freedom for some companies that do not appreciate the value we bring as employees. Everyone wants to feel appreciated.

Prior to opening my own company, I worked for a large bank as a financial advisor for almost fifteen years. I went to work for them when I was twenty-six years old, by the time I was twenty-eight years old I was a Vice-President and by the time I was thirty, I was a Senior Vice-President. I envisioned that this would be where I would work to retirement. (Yes, I had age sixty-five as my target.) My business partner and I became the number one team in the bank and we were on top of the world until it came crashing down. In July 2009, I was called into my sales manager office, put on the phone with human resources, and fired.

The backstory is that I was going through a divorce and rather than take care of the things I needed to take care of, I stuck my head in the sand. I bounced several checks over a brief period due to being depressed (not about the marriage ending but having two young children and how the divorce would affect them). I should have known better as a financial advisor. However, I'd never experienced depression before. The bank had every right to fire me, but when I needed my work family to put their arms around me and help me, they fired me. I'll never forget being escorted from the building by my sales manager, my head bowed in defeat. However, by the time I reached my car, my head was high. I knew from that point forward a big corporation would never be in control of my future.

Control Your Path

For twenty-four years, I have seen couples set their retirement goal at sixty-five years old and never question it. It's the way most people think. Why? "Because that is what everyone else is doing" or "That is what I have always been taught to focus on." Our thoughts are shaped and influenced by others as we travel through our lives. By our parents, friends, co-workers, advertisers, and society in general. If you keep listening, then you are destined to follow the same path as everyone else. When are you going to start thinking for yourself?

You control your future and the path you take. Once you realize you have the power to make a change, that's when you start looking at the world differently.

The perfect setup for retiring early is no debt, an income stream (preferably from multiple sources), a good amount of assets, and a frugal lifestyle. But what if you don't have any of these things? Can you still retire early? The answer is absolutely.

When I first started thinking about "selling everything and running away across the country," I'd dream about getting an old VW Westphalia and heading out west and living like a nomad. I quickly realized that, being 6'6", a VW Westphalia might not be the most comfortable mode of transportation for me.

However, I do fantasize about getting an old Greyhound bus, box truck, school bus, 6x6 military truck or cargo van and fixing it up as a camper and taking off. So, what does this have to do with lifestyle? The reason I bring these up is that there are folks out there living this lifestyle and doing it on a very modest budget. It's common to see a couple who converted a van or box truck or bought an old RV, fixed it up, and are now living their dream. Their budget is often $1000–$2000 a month.

It's about freedom and not being trapped by your $3000 a month mortgage and your $600 a month car payment. Many people say they prefer living a simpler life, but many times what they say and how they live just do not compute. What do we really need? What are the absolute essential items we need to live? If I had 5 minutes to get stuff out of my home because there was a fire in the basement, I'd make sure my kids and animals are out first, I'd grab the home movies, the art my children drew for me over the years, and as many pictures of my children as I could. I'm not the type to have a favorite piece of furniture or keepsake. My furnishings are just stuff to me with no real value.

Retiring early is about getting out and seeing and doing the things you want to do, while you're at an age to do them. If you plan on retiring at fifty-five years old but have no plans to do anything other than watch *Price Is Right* every morning and cut the grass every three days, then why are you retiring?

I always seem to be in a hurry. I drive fast, I eat fast, and sometimes I talk fast. Friends have commented throughout my life, "Gaddy, why are you always in a hurry?" My stock answer has always been, "Because

Now it's true that there are some great employers such as New Belgium Brewing. Talk about taking care of their employees! They cover employees' healthcare 100 percent, give two weeks paid vacation the first year, and a 5 percent match on their 401k. On your first-year anniversary you get a bike and on your fifth year you get a trip to Belgium. If that isn't enough, the employees own 100 percent of the company. They get a free shift beer, which seals the deal for me.

One telltale sign that a company takes care of their employees is when a ESOP (Employee Stock Ownership Plan) is in place. An ESOP is a company benefit that allows employees to own shares in the company. It's a great way for employers to incentivize their employees.

I'm trying to cram in as much as I can in this lifetime as possible." I've always answered people that way and never really thought about it until recently. As you get older, it's natural to start wondering why you think or do things that you do. For me, I look back and the seeds were planted early on to look at retiring early because at the end of the day, I'm still trying to cram as much into this life as possible. Those ten years between sixty-five and seventy-five years old are just not enough for me. Of course, others may be satisfied with what they have done in their lives. More power to them. I am not. And, dear reader, if you are thinking about retiring early to do something you long to do, then you are not satisfied either.

Action Plan

Many times, we are so focused on the distant future that we lose sight of what's important. Don't put a price tag on your freedom. Don't fall into the trap of "What will my friends and family think if we take off and live a non-traditional lifestyle?" Society puts pressure on us to live a certain way. Live your own life and start caring less of what society thinks. Get out there and have some fun and make memories. Life is short. So, for today:

- ✓ Track your spending—how much money goes toward necessities and how much money goes toward stuff.
- ✓ Take time to plan your early retirement. Most people spend more time planning their vacation each year than they do working on their retirement. Retiring early takes a lot of planning so don't rush it. You want to get it right.
- ✓ Think about your lifestyle now. How will you need to adjust it for you to retire early?
- ✓ Think about the lifestyle you want in retirement. Develop a budget for retiring early before you retire.
- ✓ Take care of your health. What bad habit can you give up today for a brighter tomorrow?

PART TWO

Things to Consider for Early Retirement

I have learned over the years that when one's mind is made up, this diminishes fear; knowing what must be done does away with fear.

—Rosa Parks

In this section we are going to explore several areas that you'll need to consider when you plan on retiring early. Planning out your early retirement is critical to enjoying a successful retirement.

When you sit down to plan your early retirement, healthcare will be one of the first areas you'll want to consider. Healthcare has the potential to alter your course in retirement due to cost. Healthcare can be one of your largest expenses when you start budgeting for retirement especially if you still have young children. It's expensive to cover the cost of healthcare for one or two adults, but when you start pricing out costs for a family of five, the numbers start skyrocketing. You'll want to get a handle on these costs quickly.

Social security is another area you'll want to consider. However, if you're retiring at forty-five years old, social security might not be at the top of your list of priorities but you want to consider the impact of retiring early on your future social security payments. People tend to focus on today and a year or two down the road and oftentimes social security will be overlooked. It's very important when you are budgeting to look at today, next week, next month, next year, and five, ten, fifteen, and twenty-plus years down the road.

Plan, plan, and then plan some more. It's important to have a plan in place before you just get fed up and walk into your boss's office and quit. You'll need a financial plan and a budget. You'll need a plan to communicate your early retirement plans with your family and friends. You'll want to have a plan B in case your plans don't go as planned.

Planning will take some of the fear and anxiety out of your decision to retire early. Let's say your plan is to sell everything and hit the high seas aboard your sailboat. The first week out, you shred the sails and it costs you a small fortune to get new ones. You'll probably be disappointed and a bit annoyed, but if you've done your planning, something like this shouldn't be totally unexpected.

Plan for the unexpected and hopefully it doesn't occur, but, if it does, you're prepared. Such as with healthcare, a little planning now can help offset some of the stress and anxiety later if something were to arise.

Read on to learn more.

CHAPTER FIVE

Healthcare

A mind is a terrible thing to waste.

—Arthur Allen Fletcher, Republican Civil Rights Activist

One of the big, if not the biggest hurdle in retiring early is the cost of health insurance. Even prior to the Affordable Care Act, health insurance costs were an obstacle when you decided to retire prior to sixty-five years old. Unless you were covered under your employer's healthcare plan in retirement, you would have to shop for your own private coverage. Back in those days, if you were healthy, the premiums on healthcare insurance were reasonable. If you were not healthy, then the cost of private health insurance was high. High enough to prevent many people from living out their dreams of retiring early and almost forcing them to work to sixty-five, which is when they could get on Medicare.

Since the Affordable Care Act (ACA) was passed in March 2010, the good news is that more people are covered for health insurance. The unwelcome news is that costs are rising at a steady pace and it's starting to price people out of health insurance. It seems like weekly, we are hearing about another insurance company pulling out of the marketplace. For example, Aetna and Humana recently announced they are completely leaving the ACA marketplace in 2018. Less competition often creates higher prices.

I've always looked at health insurance as a four-ring circus. In one ring are the doctors and the hospitals. In the second ring, you have the pharmaceutical companies. In the third ring, you have the lawyers. In the fourth ring, you have the insurance companies and the government. The doctors and the hospitals are at the mercy of the insurance companies and the government (Medicaid) on how much they can get reimbursed for the services they perform. On the other hand, pharmaceutical and biotech companies drive up the costs of their products. The lawyers help increase the costs because they file lawsuits, which in many cases are justified and other times frivolous. This ratchets up the cost of malpractice insurance for doctors and hospitals.

To bring down the costs of health insurance, you just can't say, "If my doctor charged me less" or "Those damn drug companies are charging way too much" or "Screw all the lawyers" or "The insurance companies are all evil." Because, in this circus, every area has contributed to the rising healthcare costs. So, you would need all four rings to agree to *lower* the cost of healthcare.

Listen, I'm 6'6" and deemed overweight by the BMI charts, plus I love smoking cigars and drinking a cold beer so I'm not picking on anyone here. But, as a society, we aren't the healthiest bunch of folks. A sizable portion of our society is overweight, a lot of us eat like crap and we exercise too little. So, most of us aren't doing anyone any favors when it comes to taking care of our own health

Think about it this way. In America, processed foods are cheaper than fruits and vegetables. It's cheaper to drop into a

HEALTHY BODY

We only have one life and one body, so we should be mindful how we treat it. When we take care of our body through exercise, eating and drinking in moderation, and getting enough sleep, our body can last us for a very long time. With proper nutrition, it will give us the proper fuel to propel us to our next adventure.

fast food restaurant and fill up on non-healthy foods than it is to go to the grocery store and buy healthy fruits and veggies. Take the countries in Central America. You can go to the city market and buy fruits and veggies much cheaper than what you'll pay for the processed foods they sell in the grocery stores. That might be a contributing factor to why health insurance in Central America is much cheaper than it is in America.

I know I'm guilty of taking the quick and easy way to getting lunch and dinner. But quick and easy generally isn't healthy and I think as a nation, quick and easy solutions for meals has become all too common and that is why we have a large obese population (myself included). Being overweight causes more health issues, such as high blood pressure and high cholesterol. When you have a large part of the population overweight, then that stresses the healthcare system. As a result, that can indirectly cause prices to increase. If you think about it, we as Americans contribute to the higher costs as well.

So how do you retire early and still have health insurance?

If you are lucky enough to retire from a job that covers you for health insurance, consider yourself fortunate. Like pensions, healthcare coverage in retirement is disappearing rapidly.

With some employers, it's possible for you to set up a more mobile lifestyle, work from the road, and remain covered with health insurance. While technically, you're not retired, you do have more freedom plus benefits. Freedom with benefits is not an unpleasant situation in a lot of cases.

If you have health insurance and you leave your job, you may be eligible for COBRA, which stands for Consolidated Omnibus Budget Reconciliation Act. COBRA allows you to have continuous coverage of health insurance for 18 months after leaving your job. Generally, COBRA is expensive, but it will keep you covered, giving you time to shop around for other options.

Buying a private policy is also expensive. However, you will have choices such as the gold policy (the most expensive but covers you the best), silver policy, and bronze policy (the cheapest but less coverage). There are also catastrophic policies that only cover major healthcare events.

Under the Affordable Care Act, you're able to shop for policies within the exchanges and, depending on your income, you may get subsidies to offset some of the costs. Due to the insurance companies pulling out of the exchanges across the country, it's becoming more of a challenge to find the coverage you seek at a reasonable price.

Another option is faith-based health sharing plans. These plans are organized by religious principles where members share in the cost of healthcare coverage. Some of the organizations offering these types of plans are Medi-Share, Liberty HealthShare, and Samartian, to name a few. The prices of the plans can be quite reasonable.

If you are planning to travel the country full time, one healthcare area that is gaining a lot of traction is Telemedicine. For a monthly charge, you have access to doctors and nurses by phone, online, or even in with some companies, video conferencing. There are currently over 200 telemedicine networks in the United States and 31 states that mandate that private insurance companies treat a telemedicine appointment as if it were an in-person visit. Before you go searching for a national network, check with your own doctor or local hospital to see if they have a telemedicine network in place. Here is a link to Freedom Telemedicine, which will give you an example of the services and

HEALTHY MIND

"A mind is a terrible thing to waste" is never truer than in our older years. Often, people retire with no goal or aim of how to keep busy, so they quickly deteriorate. Doctors often tout one of the keys to longevity as a healthy mind—mental stimulation improves brain function, which helps reduce the risk of cognitive decline and its related diseases. So, feed your mind just as you feed your body. I believe in lifelong learning—challenge your brain. It's never too late to learn a new language, play an instrument, or create some art. Utilize your brain in other ways and unlock its full potential.

costs available: https://www. freedomtelemedicine.com.

Many of the major pharmacy chains are opening quick clinics that allow you to be seen for minor medical services. Much like Urgent Care Clinics, these are not substitutes to an emergency room if there is a major medical issue, but they can handle many of your minor issues that pop up.

> **HEALTHY SPIRIT**
>
> Many believe in a spirit or soul, and that our soul has a journey and that journey is to live with purpose. So, think about what speaks to you—there will be others of like spirit. Create a community or perhaps find one that already exists and get involved. Set time aside for yourself, whether it's fifteen minutes of daily meditation, yoga, or reading, you need "me" time to decompress and escape the hustle and bustle of daily living. So, practice some self-love every day, your spirit will thank you.

Health Savings Account

Health Savings Accounts (HSA) offer some tax benefits if you have a high deductible healthcare plan. In 2018, as an individual, you're able to contribute $3,450 ($1,000 more if you are over age 55), and as a family you're able to contribute $6,900. Contributions are tax deductible and earnings are tax deferred and the distributions to pay for qualified medical expenses are tax-free. The unused balances roll-over year after year, so you won't lose the balance if you are not using it.

A Health Savings Account is a great account to add to if you plan on retiring early. It would be beneficial to start one of these plans several years before retiring so the balance can grow.

Your employer might offer you a Flex Spending account. A Flex Spending Account allows you to save money, tax-free, for any out of pocket medical expenses. It's a great plan if you plan to keep working, but if you are deciding whether to retire early or not, it does have its downside. If you leave your job, you can't take this account with you. The money you put in the account needs to be used that year, and it cannot be rolled over to the next year.

Double Check Your Plan

Not all healthcare plans are the same and not all states look at your healthcare plan like your own state. Be aware, the plan you have, say in North Carolina, might not cover you in Nevada. There are plans that, once you step outside your own state, will charge you out-of-network costs if you are not being treated in your home state. Be sure to investigate your plan before beginning your travels.

I reached out to a U.S. Congressman's office to see about getting some time on his calendar to discuss the current state of our healthcare system. I was shocked (sarcasm) when my request was routed through three different staff members, and I never received a response. It was obvious that they didn't want to touch this topic.

Retirement, Medical Issues, and Long-term Care

Whether retiring early or not, a major medical issue is the one item that can derail any retirement plan. Regardless of how much money you have saved, one major medical event can leave your retirement plan in shambles.

My sister Carol died at age fifty-one of breast and brain cancer. She had worked as a federal agent with the USDA and had a good medical plan. However, she was not ready for the numerous bills that her plan didn't cover. I'm talking about several hundred thousand worth of medical bills and she was on the hook for a good portion of that. She was already battling for her life only to go to the mailbox and see bill after bill. She didn't have the money to pay the bills and it put undue stress on her at a time she least needed it.

I recently chatted with an expat who lives in Thailand. He said that open heart surgery in Thailand costs around $16,000 in U.S. dollars, performed by U.S. trained doctors. If you get the same surgery in the United States, you'll pay over $250,000. The medical industry is big business in the United States.

If it were me, I'd fly to a foreign country to get medical care. But, if it were one of my children, I might look at it differently. So, it's all about perspective. How do you look at things—for yourself and for your loved ones.

I get asked a good bit about long-term care insurance and whether I'd recommend it? A long-term care policy can help cover some or all the cost if you needed care either at home or in a long-term care facility. I'm forty-eight years old and my immediate thoughts are not when I get older and might need care. Right now, I'm telling my kids that when I get old and sick, that I'm moving in with them and they can take care of me. (They give me the eyeroll.)

Much like most insurance plans, the hard part is that you never really know if you will need it. The younger you are, the better price you'll get on buying a long-term care plan. It can certainly pay off if you do need it in the future. Just ask a baby boomer who is taking care of a parent(s) right now. They will sing the praise of LTC plans.

If you don't have a LTC plan and a medical disaster hits, it can bankrupt you quickly. Buying a LTC policy really is a personal choice. In the early days of LTC insurance, the products that were available gave you a benefit, but you either used it or lost it at death if it was never used. Today, there are LTC policies that if you need it, you have the coverage. If you don't use it, then your family will get the money back at your death. With some LTC plans, you can cash in your plan and get your money back at a certain time, so if you change your mind about having the policy, you can get out of it. They have become, what I consider, much more "user friendly."

Rough Waters Ahead

Our healthcare choices are evolving and changing, it seems, daily. The ACA is under attack, insurance companies are pulling out of exchanges, people are dropping coverage because they can no longer afford it, and it just seems like the whole medical industry is under construction.

The good news is that there are more options coming onboard than ever before. Quick clinics in pharmacies, telemedicine options, and faith-based sharing health plans are popular options that Americans are turning to. The key is to do your homework and spend some time evaluating your choices to see what option is best for you and your family.

Action Plan

Healthcare is a personal choice and one often based on risk tolerance. We cannot look into the future to see how much healthcare we would need so we guestimate on coverage.

- ✓ Become more involved in your overall health: mind, body, and spirit.
- ✓ Think about how much health coverage you need—are you a risk taker or not a risk taker?
- ✓ Can you benefit from a Health Savings Account (HSA)?
- ✓ Do your homework: evaluate numerous plans before choosing one.

CHAPTER SIX

Social Security

Half our life is spent trying to find something to do with the time we have rushed through life trying to save.

—Will Rogers

As we discussed in the Income chapter, social security provides us a lifetime guaranteed income, which, along with pensions and annuities, are the only programs that do this. Social security is an important part of your planning process because even though you might be retiring at age fifty, you still want to ensure that you plan for what you can expect to receive in social security payments.

I'd suggest you go to www.ssa.gov/myaccount/ and sign up to view your account with social security. It's easy to log-in and get all your detailed information from when you are eligible to start taking your payments as well as how much your payments will increase if you delay taking your payments.

If you are retiring early, be sure that you have at least forty credits to qualify for social security. This is based on the idea that you have worked and paid into social security for ten years, as you will receive four credits for each year you have worked. In 2018, you'll have to

SOCIAL SECURITY
A pay-as-you-go government insurance program, which supplies benefits to retired people or those who are unemployed or disabled.

earn $1320 in income to gain one credit so for the year you'll need to have $5280 of income to gain 4 credits. By gaining the total of forty credits, this will qualify you to receive Medicare part A for free when you reach age sixty-five.

Should you delay your Social Security payment?

When you reach full-retirement age for social security, every year you delay your payment, your social security check increases by 8 percent. So, this creates a great benefit to delay taking payments until you are age seventy. At age seventy, it no longer benefits you to delay your benefit as you'll no longer receive any increases.

Why is it a benefit to delay? If you are married and your spouse has the higher social security payment, it might benefit that spouse delaying their payment to build up to a higher amount especially if there is a big age difference. At death, the surviving spouse can claim the higher social security payment. If you are single, then it might benefit you to take your benefit early.

Should you take Social Security early?

As a financial advisor, I got this question all the time. My answer has been the same for twenty-four years, "If you absolutely need it, turn it on. If you don't need it, then delay it and let it build." The breakeven point with social security is around seventy-eight years old. Hypothetically speaking, that means if you live beyond age seventy-eight, then you should have delayed your payment. If you don't live to seventy-eight years old, then you made the right decision to turn on your social security early. Since we really can't predict our longevity, the breakeven point doesn't matter as it's just a rule of thumb.

If you are still working and have not reached full-retirement age, be aware that if you are receiving your social security, in 2018 you can earn $17,040 and not be taxed on your social security. If you go over that amount, you will have $1 withheld from your payment for every $2 you earn over the $17,040 limit. So whenever possible, try to delay taking your social security if you are still working and earning more than the allowed amount. The amount does increase slightly each year.

How does early retirement affect your Social Security?

I reached out to a buddy of mine who is a specialist in social security for the answer. Don Deans is the managing director and tax strategist for Deans Consulting. Don has been a CPA for over forty years and co-wrote the book *Social Security Roadmap*.

I asked Don to explain the effects of social security if someone decides to retire at age fifty.

"If someone retires before 'normal' retirement age, their social security may be negatively impacted. Each situation is different. However, this is how social security benefits are computed. The wage earners top thirty-five years of earnings are used to compute the base used to compute the wage earners benefit. If an individual does not have thirty-five years of earnings, then the difference between their actual earning years and thirty-five is computed using zero. For example, if Mary had twenty years of earnings, this would go into the computation along with fifteen zeros.

"Additionally, the wage earner typically earns more in the later years than in their early twenties. This would also negatively impact their social security benefit.

"Before jumping to conclusions, contact your local social security office to see what your benefit at full-retirement age would be. This should only be one factor in determining whether to retire early. Get a copy of your social security statement and see if the shortage of working years will make a material difference in your decision. I would bet it would not."

Here is an example of how it would affect someone who is retiring early after working only twenty-five years not the full thirty-five years social security calculates.

Your Average Indexed Monthly Earnings (AIME) is your monthly average income over thirty-five years. It's an inflation adjusted number used to calculate your highest thirty-five years of earnings.

Let's say you started your career earning $50,000. Social security calculates an inflation increase each year but for the benefit of this example, we're going to say you received increases (raises) over the years so it will keep the indexed wages flat.

We start by taking the number of years you worked and multiplying it by your earnings (25 years x $50,000 = $1,250,000).

Then divide that number by 420. The 420 represents the number of months in 35 years: $1,250,000 / 420 = $2,976.19.

Now there is another set of numbers to pass the $2,976.19 through. Think of it as leveling the playing field for lower wage earners versus higher wage earners. This is called a replacement rate.

The first amount up to $885	90%
Amount between $885 and $5,336	32%
Amount over $5,336	10%

So, for the first $885 in earnings, multiply that by 90 percent. Then for the remaining $2,091.19, you'll multiply that by 32 percent.

$$885 \times .90 = \$796.50$$
$$\$2,091 \times .32 = \$669.18$$

For a total of **$1,465.68**—the amount you would receive at full social security age, based on paying into social security for twenty-five years and retiring early.

How about if you worked for the full thirty-five years at the same wage? Your social security would be **$1,846.63**.

By working ten more years, it would increase your full social security by 20 percent or $380.95 a month. The question you must ask yourself: Is giving up ten years of freedom worth giving up $380.95 a month in social security?

So, your social security will be impacted, but do you let that slow you down from retiring early? Not at all, but you want to make sure you gather all the information to make an informed decision.

On my social security statement, I show a thirty-year work history. However, the early ones are from when I worked at McDonald's and Pizza Hut in high school and Pinehurst Resort in college. If I continued to work until age sixty-five, those early years would be replaced by the more recent years of higher income and would increase my overall social security payment. Is it worth it to me to work until I'm sixty-five years old? No way. I'll sacrifice a few hundred dollars a month to gain the freedom I crave.

So, let's summarize. If you retire early, you may have a reduction in your social security benefits. Would you trade off retiring at age fifty-five and losing possibly a few hundred dollars in monthly social security benefits at age sixty-seven, or will you continue to work until you are sixty-seven years old to build up your social security?

Keep in mind, if you retire from your corporate job but continue to work even if it's part-time, you'll continue to pay into social security. Chances are you may not be earning as much as you were in your career, so your social security might still decline. It just won't decline as much if you are still contributing something toward it versus being completely retired.

Is Social Security Going Broke?

Social security does have some issues. If you received your social security statement in the mail this year, you likely saw the following statement: **"The law governing benefit amounts may change because, by 2034, the payroll taxes collected will be enough to pay only about 79 percent of scheduled benefits."**

Social security is being stressed due to our population living much longer than we did thirty years ago. When social security was first put in place in the 1930s, the full-retirement age then was age sixty-five. Back in the 1930s, people weren't living many years beyond age sixty-five. Today, it's common to live into your nineties and collect twenty-plus years of social security checks.

Also, with the baby boom generation racing toward age sixty-five, there is a large part of our population who will be covered by social security. This puts added stress on the program.

Based on the Social Security Administration's message on our statements about not having enough to pay only 79 percent in 2034, should you be concerned?

Let me assure you, social security is not going away. Could your benefit be reduced? I doubt it. Congress can fix this problem with the stroke of a pen. That might include tax increases as we get closer to 2034 to help close the gap of what is collected in payroll taxes and what is needed to pay out the benefit. It also could include raising the social security age of when you are eligible to receive the benefit. This is a very important benefit to people and one that I do not see going away or being reduced.

Action Plan

- ✓ Set up an account with social security and check your numbers.
- ✓ Check with your local social security office to see if they can calculate the effect of your early retirement on your current numbers.
- ✓ Factor your social security payments into your long-term income plan.
- ✓ If you are married, delaying your benefit on the highest earning spouse might benefit you while you turn the other spouse's benefit on early.
- ✓ If you are single, it might benefit you to turn on social security early.

CHAPTER SEVEN

Planning for Retirement

Every adversity, every failure, every heartache carries with it the seed of an equal or greater benefit.

—Napoleon Hill

So, you want to retire early. What are you going to do? If you're not going to travel, then how are you going to keep yourself from being bored "out of your mind"? Perhaps you can turn a hobby into your next business. I often see people follow their passions and create great businesses. Woodworking is a good example of how someone takes a hobby and turns it into a successful business. What's not to like about this? You control how much you want to work, when the project will be completed, and how much time you want to put into it. You don't have some bully of a boss screaming at you, setting deadlines, or threatening your job. You are in complete control, doing exactly what you want to be doing. Retiring early is all about gaining your freedom back. Seize the day.

How Will Retiring Early Affect Those Around You?

Let's say you plan on retiring at fifty-six years old, but it will be another five years before your spouse can retire. This can cause some friction in the family. My best advice is to make sure you are both on the same page when it comes to retiring, whether you are retiring early or not. I've had clients who up and quit their job on a random day. It was almost like they hit that breaking point and just couldn't take another day. Their spouses weren't very happy with them.

When I met my life partner, Deb, eight years ago, she was working 60–70 hours a week as a process engineer in manufacturing. We'd compare notes on the "personalities" we worked with. I'd mention that I worked with a couple of "ass kissers" at the bank and she would point out one or two at her workplace. She'd mention the "insecure bullies" she worked with, and I could name two or three who I worked with. We each could name "backstabbers" and so on. It seems every workplace has these personalities, and they are just part of society. For several years, Deb and I would sit around and say, "To hell with these places, we need to get out and do something different." At the end of the day, we both got fired, because when you start opening your mouth and standing up for yourself or stating your opinion, some places do not like that and find a way to get

I knew this couple where the husband was sixty-three years old and had worked for GM for forty years and his wife was a homemaker. For forty years their routine was the same, the husband would leave at 7:30am and would return at 5:30pm. His wife had her own routine through the week, which she had done for years. So, when the husband announced that he was retiring at the end of the year, his wife stated: "Congratulations on your retirement. However, I want you to know that even though you might not have a job at the end of the year, I'm still going to pack you a lunch like I do every day and you'll leave this house at 7:30am like you do during the week and you'll not be allowed back in this house before 5:30pm." She added: "You might be retiring but you're not going to affect my routine and my schedule." His answer was, "Heck, if I'm barred from the house, I might as well continue to work." And he did, for another four years.

rid of you. In my case, I gave them a reason. For years I had wanted to open my own firm and leave the big corporate bank behind, but I was too fearful of doing so. It took a kick in the pants (getting fired) for me to get out and pursue my dream. With that said, it's always better to go out on your terms because that gives you time to get your Plan B in place.

Always Have a Plan B

When I was in college, I worked at the Pinehurst Hotel in Pinehurst, NC, as a doorman. This is where I encountered the best piece of advice that I have ever been given. As a young college student, I'd run across businessmen coming to Pinehurst to play golf from all over the world. One day I was chatting it up with a fellow from England and I asked him (just like I asked many other businessmen): "What is the best advice you could give to a college student studying business?" His answer: "Always have a plan B. No matter how well your career is going, always have a plan B."

So, what is a plan B? Plan B is your backup plan or an alternative route that you might take if you are forced or *need* to go in a different direction in your career. Your plan B might be putting your D.I.A.L. in motion and leaving your career. It could be exiting your corporate career to finally buy or start your own business. Plan B is formed when you say to yourself: "If my current position does not work out, then I'll go do this other thing." The "other thing" is your plan B. I always felt comfortable knowing that I had a plan B, C, and D in case my current job didn't work out.

Warren Buffet

Warren Buffet is the most successful investor of all-time with a net worth of reportedly 75 billion dollars. What I find fascinating is that Mr. Buffet still lives in the same home he purchased for $31,500 back in 1958. Today, that same home is worth an estimated $650,000.

Mr. Buffet can afford to buy himself an entire island to live on if he wanted to or a building overlooking Central Park in New York City, so why would he live in the same home for the last fifty-nine years in Omaha, Nebraska? In interviews over the years, he's mentioned that this is where he is happiest and why would he need ten houses around the world. At his core, Mr. Buffet is a frugal man, who has made smart and shrewd investments. Oh, by the way, he announced in recent years that he plans to donate 99 percent of his wealth to charity. Would Warren Buffet have found the same success if he had lived a life of extravagance? Perhaps, but my bet would be that he wouldn't have been as successful if he owned a fleet of planes and exotic cars.

Communicate Your Early Retirement Plan

The key in retiring early as a couple is communication. Getting on the same page can be difficult at times especially when it comes down to changing your lifestyle.

Here is an idea of the thought process needed to communicate effectively with each other about retiring early. Of course, if you're not going to travel, then it doesn't matter if both spouses retire together.

1. Is retiring early something that appeals to you both? I've met some folks who absolutely love their career and find rising through the ranks at their company very satisfying. So, if your spouse is one of these folks, it might be more difficult to even enter the conversation about retiring early. If you're single, then it makes the conversation much easier: You decide.

2. So, you're both on the same page about retiring early. Now, you must figure out if you can or not. Is it financially feasible for you to do so? This is where the real work comes into play. Using the D.I.A.L. method in this book should give you a good picture of where you are currently. Then you can go to your CPA, financial advisor, or (shameless plug) contact us

at www.retireearly365.com to find assistance in determining whether you can retire early or not.

3. Financially, you find out that it's going to work for you. Now it's time to determine what you are going to do in retirement. This is where you and your spouse must agree on your retirement lifestyle. You want to sell your home and move into a cabin in Wyoming and live off-grid. However, your spouse wants to move to Costa Rica and live near the ocean. Something must give. Deciding the direction of your plans in retirement might take some compromise. For example, I sold Deb on the idea of taking off in the RV for a few years. (She claims this was her idea, so I let her own it.) I've not done a respectable job of selling her on the idea of moving to Mexico or another foreign country after the RVing. When we talk about Yellowstone or the Grand Canyon she's all smiles. When I bring up Mexico or Thailand, I get this cockeyed look from her which indicates to me that I have some more selling to do, or perhaps more thinking on my part: what can I compromise on?

4. So now you're both on the same page with retiring early. Financially you are set, and you've determined your future. Now what? Now it's time to set a date to retire from your career. Life as you know it is about to change.

5. It's time to start putting your plans in place. Let's say your plans are to downsize to a tiny home. You'll need to identify where you're going to build your home, design your new home, and look to sell your old home. You'll probably need to hold a few yard sales to downsize your furnishings to prepare for your move. Unless you are staying put in your current home, prepping for your new freedom will take time.

Presuming that you have planned thoroughly to get to early retirement, you don't want to have those plans go up in flames by making poor financial choices. Once you retire from your career, the plan is for you to stay retired and not have to return to that career.

Here are some suggestions to keep you on track.

1. Continue to have a budget in retirement. You don't want your monthly expenses suddenly drifting higher and higher each month. Track what you are spending so you can adjust if you need to.

2. If you plan on buying a RV, moving to a foreign country, buying a pair of Harley Davidson motorcycles or a boat, etc., be sure to do your homework before you buy. Could you save some money if you buy used or bought something smaller? Too many people buy on impulse and that's where people lose a good bit of money. Think through your decisions and do your homework.

3. Always have an emergency fund. The next surprise is right around the corner and you want to be prepared for when it happens.

4. Watch out for family members. A major medical expense is probably the number one retirement plan destroyer. However, needy grown kids and family members rank right up there as another retirement plan wrecker. I've had clients who nearly let their children bankrupt them because every time the children needed money, Mom and Dad whipped out their checkbook and solved their problem for them.

   I've had a couple of clients tell me that they just can't say no to their family members and children, so they give them what they ask for. They want to say no but feel obligated to give out money. My response is: "Okay, from now on, you are going to blame your lack of money on me, your financial advisor. Going forward, when a family member asks for money, you're going to tell them that your $^@$& financial advisor has your money locked down and you are not able to give them any money." I tell them to have the family member call me if they need money that bad. Emergencies are one thing but, at the end of the day, you are not a bank where family and grown kids can make withdrawals.

Now there are legit cases where you want to help your children when there is a real need. I'm not talking about these cases. I'm talking about the son and daughter who can't keep a job. They work a part-time job but expect you to be the full-time babysitter for your grandchildren. There are children out there who think nothing of taking every dime from their parents. I have a client in her eighties who is on the verge of bankruptcy because her son is milking her dry. It's sad. As parents we must accept our role in the decisions as well. Nobody knows your children better than you do. Ninety-eight percent of the time, there are no issues from the kids but if you have one of the other 2 percent, watch out and be aware.

5. BE FRUGAL, BE FRUGAL, BE FRUGAL! You need your money to last many years. If you are not frugal, research on how to become frugal. Change your mindset and start looking at your spending habits differently. What do all of us really need? A roof over our heads, food in our belly, love and happiness.

Pros and Cons to Retire Early

What are the Pros and Cons to retiring early? Another way to look at it is, what is the net positive to retiring early?

Pros
- Freedom: You choose to do what you want to do, when you want to do it.
- You have gained the ability to travel because your job no longer anchors you where you live now.

- You have more time to spend with your children and create even more awesome memories than you already have.
- You have time to think, reflect, and grow as a person versus being so busy with your job that you can't even think straight anymore.
- You can do the things that you always wanted to do but never had time to. Things such as grow a garden, get in the best shape of your life, read Tolstoy's *War & Peace* (all 1225 pages of it), or try out a new hobby.
- You have the time to create. Perhaps you've been thinking about starting an online business or tinkering with an idea you might want to get a patent on. Now you have the time to focus and not be distracted.

Cons

- You'll have to be even more mindful and disciplined with your money. There is no paycheck coming once you walk away from your career. However, that doesn't mean you can't create one.
- Your family might not understand the decision. Unless everyone in your family is on the same page with you retiring early, things can get a bit tense. Surprising your kids one day by announcing that Mom and Dad are retiring early, selling the house, and moving to Costa Rica to live out the rest of your lives might not go over so well. Communication is key.
- You lose your identity. Especially for men, we tend to identify with what we do for a career. Think about it, if you put a group of guys who have never met each other in a room, normally one of the first few questions is: "What do you do for a living?" Now, I'm the first to say that I'd be happy to announce, "I'm retired." Some folks are going to struggle with losing their "identity" because they no longer have a career. So, create a new identity. I assure you, if you answer the question "What do you do for a living?" with "I retired

at forty-eight years old and now I travel the country touring all the National Parks," you just became a lot more interesting than saying, "I'm Larry and I'm an accountant."

- You might have to downsize. The kids are off on their own and now you and your spouse are sitting in a three-thousand-square-foot home. You find yourselves only using one bedroom, one bath, the kitchen, and the den. The rest of the house is being used to store your stuff and you rarely use the other rooms. You find that you can't retire early with the large mortgage payment due every month. Many folks choose to sell the larger home and move into a much smaller home, maybe even a tiny home. Think about it, if you're only using four rooms in your house, why are you paying for the whole home? Often, folks can sell their home and take the equity and buy a much smaller house and pay it off completely. Do you own your home or does your home own you?

NEWTON'S LAW

Isaac Newton's third law of motion states: "Every action has an equal or opposite reaction." That doesn't mean that the reaction is necessarily negative, but it could be. Let's say that you and your spouse have a five-year plan to retire early. You have a budget, a plan to pay down debt, and you're building up your assets. One random Tuesday afternoon, a year into your five-year plan, you and your boss have some "words" and you are out of a job. This action has now created a negative reaction to your plan. Now your five-year plan might have just gone to seven years.

Newton's law can have a positive affect as well. You and your spouse plan to work until age sixty-five. Now you're both fifty-eight years old but due to some cutbacks at work, you lose your job. At first, the only thing you can think about is getting another job, but you've never thought about not working at least until sixty-five years old. However, you losing your job has left a bitter taste in your mouth about going back to a similar blue/white-collar job. It's opened you're eyes to the possibility of doing something completely different. You visit your financial advisor and find out that you can make do with less. You losing your job was not a "positive" but the "opposite reaction" was that it opened your mind and gave you options once you viewed your future in a different way.

> Sara gets out of pharmacy school at age twenty-five and she has a starting salary of $80,000 a year. Over the next ten years, her salary increases to $120,000 a year. By living reasonably, Sara has been able to put $3000 a month into savings/investments. Now at thirty-five, Sara has put away $36,000 a year and at a 4 percent interest rate, she has roughly $441,000 saved. If she continued another five years, she'd have $738,000 at age forty. With Sara's skill set, she could start her own online pharmacy consulting business and live out her days on the beach in Costa Rica.

Retiring Before 50

Can you retire in your early thirties? Absolutely. But unless you received an inheritance, you'll want to lay the groundwork early for retiring at, say, thirty years of age. Time is a vital component when considering retiring early because of the power of compound interest. At age thirty, there simply hasn't been enough time for compound interest to add up for you, so you'll have to save and invest your way to retiring early.

We've all heard of the high school or college student who made that incredible phone app or tech gadget and sold it for millions. But not everyone has a leg up like this. Nor does everyone have rich parents who can fund their kids into a business in their twenties, so they can sell it for millions in their thirties.

So how can the average twenty-something retire in their thirties? Living frugal and saving as much as possible is the key.

Retiring Early and College Costs

One area that can be an obstacle when it comes to retiring early is the cost of sending your children to college. Most of us with teenage children are shocked at the cost of college once you have a child old enough to start looking at their college options. The cost of going to college increases at a rate of 8 percent each year.

So how do you pull off an early retirement *and* send your kids to college? Ideally, you have put aside money for many years and the cost of college is not an issue for you. However, being a financial advisor for twenty-four years, I know this isn't the case for many people. Academic and athletic scholarships are also possible but not everyone will qualify for these.

What is the normal person to do? Here are some ideas:

> Scott is a bartender who makes about $50,000 a year. Scott is twenty-three years old and has a goal to travel the United States by the time he's thirty. He spends the next four years savings $800 a month. At twenty-seven, Scott has saved up $41,000 and hits the road in the van he converted into a camper. Along the way, he picks up seasonal bartending jobs. Scott also gets licensed to deal poker and he fills in at various casinos around the country. He's living his dream, traveling the United States and working when he wants and needs to work.

1. *Community Colleges* are great options these days. Keep in mind, generally at any university, the first two years are core classes. Unless your child is in a special program, most schools won't have them declare a major until their junior year. So why not save a considerable amount of money for the first two years, and then they can transfer to a four-year school?

2. *Use the community college system* to get residency. Out-of-state tuition can be extremely expensive. I've known parents who use the community college system in another state to send their child for two years. Then they will have in-state residency established so when they transfer to that larger four-year university in the same state, they pay in-state tuition prices.

3. *Free tuition.* Yes, some colleges offer free tuition. Tuition is free at the five U.S. military academies: The US Military Academy (West Point), US Coast Guard Academy, US Naval Academy, US Air Force Academy, and the US Merchant Marine Academy. All costs are paid for but there will be a service obligation, as a five-year minimum commitment is required. There are also public and private schools that offer free tuition for students who qualify (see https://affordableschools.net/20-tuition-free-colleges/). One overlooked area is colleges located overseas that offer free tuition to U.S. students.

4. *Free money*. These days there are millions and millions of dollars in grants and scholarships. Many have very specific guidelines to qualify, but many are also more open-ended. I have found the hard part is searching for these as they tend not to be located on one specific website. If you spend some time doing your homework, it could pay off financially.

5. *Try to stay in-state* whenever possible. There is a dramatic difference in cost when you have a student that stays in-state versus going out-of-state. There is a state university about an hour from where I live called Western Carolina University. They just dropped their tuition to $500 a semester for in-state and $2500 for out-of-state (this does not include room and board and meal plan). The state of NC recently dropped the cost at two other state universities to reflect the $500 in-state and $2500 out-of-state tuition cost. Try and stay up-to-date with price changes with your child's schools of interest.

6. *Work-study jobs*. Most colleges will allow students to get part-time jobs at their school to help offset the cost of college. These jobs could be working on or off campus such as working at the admissions office. The student will be paid directly, and then they can apply their earnings to their college bills.

Brian and Amber are both thirty-four years old and have saved $100,000 over their careers. They have two children, both under the age of ten. Amber works as a bookkeeper at a local construction company and Brian is a web designer. They both have a desire to live a more mobile lifestyle and not just sit in one spot. Brian's job is easily mobile because if he has access to a computer, cell phone, and an Internet connection, he can work anywhere in the world. Amber convinces her boss that she doesn't have to be present in the office every day for the bookkeeping to be done. Matter of fact, Amber sets up her own bookkeeping company and takes on more clients and builds a nice following on the road.

Retiring early and paying for college at the same time can be tricky. Try and spend some time researching your options. It will save you money if you do.

A growing trend is a mobile lifestyle. Increasingly, younger families are hitting the road.

Homeschooling has become mainstream especially with numerous online education options. What better way to learn about Mount Rushmore, the Grand Canyon or Niagara Falls than to take your children there and show them.

How Will Your Obituary Read?

Will it say that you worked a corporate job for forty-five years and that you loved hunting and fishing. (But you never had time to do either

Kelly is a nurse and she is thirty-nine years old. She is divorced and has one son and he's getting ready to go to college. Kelly has always wanted to travel and see various parts of the United States, but she is concerned about the cost of college and the cost of traveling. Regarding the cost of traveling, Kelly is in the perfect occupation to travel and work due to the high demand for traveling nurses. Normally, a traveling nurse will sign a 13-week temporary contract, which normally can be extended. The wages earned are very attractive and should be able to fuel Kelly's travels with ease. It also allows her to sign a 13-week contract and once finished, she could take a few weeks off and change locations and start a new 13-week contract. This is a very good option for someone with a nursing skill set.

because you were always working.) Maybe it will say that you had eight grandchildren, but you only saw them a couple of times a year because after you retired at age sixty-eight, your body started falling apart and you were unable to travel to see them. It might say that you were married to Mary for forty-seven years. Mary was your partner and the adventurous one. She wanted you to retire five years earlier so you both could travel the world. But since this isn't what you wanted and were too stubborn to compromise, Mary had to put her dreams on hold. Now that you're gone, Mary is traveling the world with her friends. Or your obituary can read: You retired at age fifty-eight and traveled the world with your wife Mary. When you weren't out adventuring, you and Mary spent your time enjoying your grandchildren and teaching them how to hunt and fish. You passed away last Friday, having lived your life to the fullest, regretting nothing.

You have one life. You can spend it working, stressing and chasing money, or you can take control and plot your own course.

You Still Have Time to Rewrite Your Story.

Many people think life is about taking the straightest road: Live in the same house for forty years, work at the same job, and live the way your parents did. Whereas other people live life on a road full of left and right turns. Nothing is predictable in their lives. We sometimes see this with military families where every few years they are uprooted and sent to another part of the country or the world.

Perhaps you have lived your life on the straight road for your first forty years. You have lived cautiously and conservatively, but you have always dreamed of something more adventurous. What is holding you back? If not now, when will you make the changes that you have dreamed about? We are all on the clock and our time is running out. Stop procrastinating and start making some left and right turns in your life.

When we think of procrastinating, it normally is in the context of putting off something we don't want to do. So why procrastinate on the things you *do* want to do? If you really want to retire at fifty-five, what (or who) is holding you back? Is it fear? Is it lack of confidence in your plan? Is your spouse not on the same page as you? Spend some time figuring out what holds you back, then look for a way to overcome it. Perhaps you've been procrastinating on a positive outcome? That trip you've always wanted to take but find excuses not to. Procrastination and excuses can leave you with regrets at the end of your life. I don't know about you, but I certainly don't want to have any regrets at the end of my life.

Action Plan

The road of life shouldn't be filled with would've, should've, could've, and didn't. Nor should it be filled with excuses and reasons why you never were able to do the things you always wanted to do but didn't. It's not too late to change your narrative. It's not too late to start making some left and right turns. It's not too late to rewrite your story.

✓ Think about at what age you want to retire, then plan to get there.
✓ What is your Plan B?
✓ What do you want to do when you retire? Make a list.
✓ Speak to your family/significant other about your early retirement plan.

CHAPTER EIGHT

The Five Estate Planning Documents Everyone Should Have

Your time is limited, so don't waste it living someone else's life. Don't be trapped by dogma—which is living with the results of other people's thinking. Don't let the noise of others' opinions drown out your own inner voice. And most important, have the courage to follow your heart and intuition.

—Steve Jobs

When I mention estate planning, most people automatically think they need to be sixty years old before they start to think of getting these documents together. This is absolutely not the case.

Throughout my career as a financial advisor, estate planning was the number one item that people procrastinated on doing. According to AARP, 60 percent of the population doesn't have a basic will nor have they done any estate planning. I've seen the difficulties of not getting documents in order. I once had a client in her fifties who was financially comfortable, but she was dying of cancer and her boyfriend took care of her. Her two sisters, whom she did not have a relation-ship with, did not approve of her boyfriend, whom the woman had been with for many years. With the potential of an inheritance, her two sisters came to town to try and get a judge to declare my client incompetent. Luckily, my client was able to prove she was mentally capable of taking care of her own affairs. She put an estate plan together to ensure she was cared for, as well as her boyfriend, after her passing. Her wants were assured before it was too late. However, I have also seen cases where a judge successfully provided guardianship over someone, putting a plan into place that was not what the person wanted. I've also seen estates go to family that the deceased had no relationship with. Having your estate documents in order can prevent this type of rogue behavior. An estate plan is a way to ensure your wants, needs, and wishes are fulfilled.

With changes to the healthcare privacy laws, it's crucial to get your documents in order. And the earlier the better, as your life and health can change even at a young age. I've just sent my eighteen-year-old daughter off to college. Because she is now legally an adult if she were to end up in the hospital, the hospital would not be able to share any information with me without written authorization. Without the proper documents, most parents would not be able to make health-care or financial decisions without going to court to get approval. Most parents automatically think that since it's their child and they are still considered dependents on their tax returns they would be able to make decisions on their behalf. In most states this is simply not the case.

Get Your Plan Together

Estate planning is a task that is easily put off. It's the thing you'll do next week, month, or year. You need to confront the inevitable. You're going to die. So, do not put off a life chore, for one day it may be too late.

Estate planning was a topic I brought up early in the client-advisor relationship. I'm not an attorney, but I helped my clients think about what they wanted to accomplish in case they ever became unable to make their own decisions. I suggested information gathering prior to meeting with an attorney to smooth the process. Clients would bring up the idea of printing off the documents online and doing it themselves. I would not suggest doing this, because you need to get these documents right. Don't trust some online fill-in-the-blanks print-off to completely accomplish your goals. Keep in mind, you're talking about the transfer of the assets you have accumulated over your lifetime. You don't want to mess this up by saving a few dollars.

> **PRINCE**
>
> In 2016, the artist formerly known as Prince died with a net worth of approximately $300 million, before taxes. Unlike Michael Jackson, who had a comprehensive estate plan, Prince did not. After Prince's death, it became known that he was a quiet giver. We may never know how much he actually gave to charity, but without putting a plan in place, he can no longer give from the grave. This means about 50 percent of his estate is going to the federal and state governments. His heirs will get the rest. What happened? Heirs came out of the woodwork, claiming to be his wife, child, or other relative. His estate will most likely go to his six siblings. It doesn't matter what relationship he had with them, the DNA connection is enough.

I suggest hiring a qualified attorney to set up your documents. What do I mean by a qualified attorney? An attorney who focuses on estate planning. Some attorneys advertise that they do estate planning, but they also do real estate closings, traffic violations, contract law, family law, bankruptcy, and so on. Find an attorney who specializes in estate planning. Oftentimes, you'll find attorneys who will offer a package that gives you all five documents for a flat fee.

Now here is the part that most people skip over. When you get your documents back from the attorney, read them to make sure everything is accurate. Last year, I had a client who passed away with a will that had a major error in it. He and his wife got their wills done at the same time. He was leaving his assets to his wife and his wife was leaving her assets to him. After he passed away, it was discovered that his will was written so that he was actually leaving his assets to himself. The attorney's office used the same template while doing his wife's will but forgot to replace his name with hers. He was his own beneficiary. This was fairly easy to overcome, but there were extra steps that had to be taken to get it corrected. His wife had enough to do and should not have had to make these extra phone calls and appointments.

I could share story after story on why getting these five documents in order is imperative. Hanging around the funeral home as a kid, there were times when I saw a family come for a visitation to mourn the death of their family member and the topic of money would come up. Next thing you know, everyone is outside raring to fight. Money and greed can bring out the worst in people. If you leave this earth without having your intentions known on how you want your assets split up, it will cause problems. Why not make it easy for your family and get the documents in place?

What Are These Five Documents?

1. Will

A will is the foundation of your plan so that's where you want to start. It allows you to delegate where you want your property and assets to go at your death.

In your will, you'll want to name someone to handle your affairs once you have passed. This person is called an executor. An executor might be your spouse, your child, or an attorney. If you don't name an executor, the court will name one. This person may or may not be the person you would have chosen. Intestate is the term used when you die without a will. When this happens, your property and assets will be distributed based on the laws of the state in which you passed away in. I don't know about you, but I certainly don't want the state to be in charge of where my assets are going. This is why it's important to get a will.

Some common mistakes people make with their wills:

1. Doing it themselves and leaving out key items.

2. Leaving out their businesses—people often focus on all the other areas of their

> ### DESIGNATE A BENEFICIARY
>
> This is very important. Your will might state that you want to leave everything to your spouse. But your IRA has your children as your beneficiaries. Who gets the IRA in the scenario? The children will because who you name as a beneficiary on your retirement accounts or annuities will always trump what the will states. Be sure to double check who you have listed as your beneficiary and make sure it matches your will if that is what you want.

personal life and forget to add their business into their will.

3. Not updating their will after life changes. Throughout our lives, we might experience divorces, children getting married, grandchildren being born, or the loss of a spouse. It's extremely important to keep your will updated.

4. Not getting around to writing a will. "I'll get to it one day." Well one day might be too late. You want to get on this now. If you have a will in place that was done some time ago, review it and have it updated where necessary.

2. Healthcare Durable Power of Attorney

A will takes care of your property and assets at your death. However, numerous problems can occur, such as becoming incapacitated.

A healthcare durable POA (also known as a healthcare proxy) allows you to name someone (you can have more than one person named) who will make medical decisions for you in the case you cannot.

Another consideration, if you choose, is to have a Do Not Resuscitate (DNR) order drawn up. This instructs medical personnel not to revive you if you were to go into cardiac arrest.

I have seen the effect of not having a healthcare durable POA firsthand. My sister was dying from cancer and wanted to live out her days in Florida with her longtime boyfriend. I kept telling her she needed to get a healthcare durable POA because our mother was not a big fan of her boyfriend. My sister never did, and my mother was able to go to court and get guardianship over my sister. At that point, my sister's boyfriend was cut out. If there was a healthcare durable POA in place, my sister would have died where and with whom she wanted.

3. Living Will

A living will (also called an advanced directive) gives you the opportunity to list, in a legal document, what your wishes are when it comes to healthcare decisions. It allows you to approve and reject certain healthcare treatments. With a Healthcare Durable POA (spoken of in number 2), you name a person(s) to carry out your medical choices. This person cannot override what is in your living will.

Often having a living will can be easier on your family because they can see what your wishes are regarding your healthcare treatment. Look at it as a gift to your loved ones. They are aware of your wants, which makes their job as a POA easier. While it is a hard discussion to have, share with the person(s) how you want to be treated in different scenarios. In addition to the legal document, that discussion is an important one to have. For example, I had a friend who had major health issues. She had a vague living will and a POA in place, but never had a verbal discussion with her POA. She loved life and loved being social. Accepting the reality of her health problems, she shared with me that she would rather move on to her next adventure than, to use her words, be put in a corner to drool on herself. At seventy years young, following a heart attack, she ended up on life support with severe brain damage. Her body was kept alive via a breathing and feeding tube. I knew this was not how she wanted to live. Her POA did not. It took five days for her POA to come to terms with making the hard decision to let her go. My friend used an online service to set up her living will. She should have been more detailed in her living will and had a discussion with her POA.

A living will does not expire until death or it is revoked by you. It will only be activated when your primary physician finds you can no longer make medical decisions on your own or if you are in an incapacitated state.

State laws vary on how living wills are handled, so it's best to check with your own state to see what is required.

4. Financial Durable Power of Attorney

With a financial durable POA, you're assigning a person(s) to handle your financial affairs in case you are unable to do so. If you're incapacitated, your bills still need to be paid and financial decisions still need to be made. The person you name in your document becomes your attorney-in-fact.

A financial durable POA goes into effect in two ways. The first is it can be in effect immediately after signing it. With married couples, they will often have financial durable POAs on each other in case something happens with one of them, the authority to take over the financial affairs is already in place. The second way is that you set it up to where it does not go into effect until a medical doctor signs off that you are in an incapacitated state.

5. HIPPA Release

The Health Insurance Portability and Accountability Act of 1996 was signed into law to insure patient's privacy when it comes to medical records. The reason to get a HIPPA Release signed is because, without it, you may not be able to access certain medical information. For example, you are named as someone's healthcare power of attorney. However, the healthcare POA is triggered only at incapacitation. If

QUALIFIED PERSONAL RESIDENCE TRUST

A Qualified Personal Residence Trust (QPRT) is a special trust that removes your primary or secondary estate from your taxable estate and saves you a significant amount of taxes in the future. When you put your primary or secondary home inside a QPRT, it locks in the value at that point so that any future appreciation does not affect your estate. Please consult an estate planning attorney to learn more.

the doctor has not deemed the patient incapacitated, they will not be able to share any medical information with you without a signed HIPPA release form. This means if your child is over eighteen years old and gets into an accident, the medical staff would not be able to share any information with you without a signed HIPPA release.

What About a Trust?

The Business Dictionary defines a trust as a "legal entity created by a party (the trustor) through which a second party (the trustee) holds the right to manage the trustor's assets or property for the benefit of a third party (the beneficiary)." A trust allows you to set up rules to be followed on the passing of the property and assets to your beneficiaries (including charities). Some of the benefits to setting up a trust are avoiding probate, helping to reduce estate taxes, and protecting assets. Here is an example. You set up a trust for your children (beneficiaries), so this makes you the trustor. A bank trust department can fill the role as the trustee—they manage your assets while you are still living or take over at your passing. It's their job to follow your trust instructions to pay out the trust to your children.

Trusts come in many different varieties all depending on what you want to accomplish. Let's say you have an irresponsible son and you know that if you died and left him with a lot of money he'd blow right through it. You could set up a trust that allows you to control the money from the grave and hand it out to him over time. I heard about a father, who owned a very large construction company, who was concerned about leaving money to his son. You see his son had never made anything of himself, couldn't keep a job, and the father suspected that his son was just waiting around for him to die in order to get a large inheritance. The father set up a trust that stated for every dollar the son made, the trust would match dollar for dollar. If the son didn't work, then the son got zero dollars from the trust. I thought this was brilliant.

IRREVOCABLE LIFE INSURANCE TRUST

An Irrevocable Life Insurance Trust (ILIT) allows you to purchase your life insurance inside a trust so that the life insurance proceeds sit outside of your estate. For example, in 2018, your lifetime exemption is $5.6 million for an individual. That means an individual can die and as long as their estate was under $5.6 million, there will be no federal estate tax or gift tax. An ILIT would allow, for example, that $1,000,000 life insurance policy not to show up in your estate. Thus, it wouldn't count against your $5.6 million. Please consult an estate planning attorney to learn more.

Not everyone needs a trust. If there are specific needs and circumstances that dictate a trust, then they are great. One thing I see repeatedly is that people spend a lot of money setting up trusts but then never fund them. Once you set up a trust, you need to rename assets into the trust's name. These assets can be your home, bank accounts and investments, real estate, etc. The trust does you no good unless you actually retitle assets in the name of the trust.

Already Have a Plan? Revisit It.

A will that you set up twenty-five years ago probably needs to be updated unless you haven't had any major changes in your life. I'd suggest still having it looked at. Financial and healthcare durable powers of attorney need to be reviewed every five years. Major life changes such as a divorce or death should have you automatically revisiting your estate plan.

Estate laws change every year, so it would be a good idea for you to monitor these changes in case there is an effect on your plan.

DID YOU KNOW...

Fees related to estate planning are tax deductible?

Having an attorney prepare a will or a medical power of attorney is not tax deductible. However, if your estate plan requires the use of a CPA or tax planner, those fees can be tax deductible. The IRS says that estate planning fees can be tax deductible for the production or collection of income, or the management of the property held for production of income, or tax advice and tax planning. Check with your CPA or tax preparer to find out if your estate planning fees can be written off.

Action Plan

You're about to embark on a different chapter in your life once you retire early. Your plans might have you traveling around the world, roaming the country in your RV, or sailing off to the Caribbean. It's extremely important that you and your family are protected in case a medical emergency develops. Even if your retiring early plan keeps you planted where you are, estate planning documents give you piece of mind— you have your affairs in order in case something happens.

Getting these documents will cost you some money, but I assure you it can save your family money and heartache in the future. Plus, you want to enjoy your early retirement, not worry about paperwork.

So, stop procrastinating and get them.

PART THREE

Live Your Life

A man is not old until regrets take the place of dreams.

—John Barrymore

Welcome to your retirement. In this section, we're going to explore some of the ways folks live when they decide to retire early. Your path might be completely different, but each of the areas we explore are gaining popularity with increasingly more people. Whether you retire at age forty or age sixty-five, you must start thinking about what you will do to keep yourself occupied. It's been my experience watching my clients over the years as they retire, if you go home and do nothing, you'll probably not live as long as someone who stays mentally and physically active. You're most likely asking for medical issues if you plant yourself in front of the TV every day.

I've had husband and wife clients who both rode Harley Davidson motorcycles. One couple had their bikes for over five years, yet they had less than a thousand miles on the bikes. They always wanted to go to Sturgis, SD, to the huge motorcycle rally, but they always had to work. They had plenty of money but had the mindset that they were going to work until they were sixty-five. I pushed them every year to take some time off and go to Sturgis, and finally they decided to do it. It was a life-altering trip for them. Having gone to Sturgis, their focus turned to wanting to go to the Grand Canyon and then to Yellowstone. The list of places grew and grew. They came into my office and asked if they could retire now, before they turned sixty-five. The numbers indicated they could. They ended up selling their business and taking off.

Retirement is the reward we receive for all the arduous work we've put into our career. Most people fantasize about what they'll do with all their spare time in retirement, especially the closer they get to retirement.

Much like our personalities are different, so are our likes and dislikes. Some of you might find riding a motorcycle down the highway relaxing and stress free, whereas other folks find nothing relaxing about riding a motorcycle.

While working at the Pinehurst Resort, in college, I had a chance to play most of the golf courses for free or at a very discounted price. Every day we had the various golf pros come to the hotel to drop off the deposits from the courses at which they worked. It wasn't too uncommon for them to offer free golf lessons if we wanted them. I never took them up on it, but I really wish I had.

Having worked in a bank for many years, bankers always tried to get me to play golf with them or join their golf team for a local tournament. Early in my career, I would. However, I was awful and didn't find the game one bit relaxing, so I gave it up. When you hit enough houses and parked cars, there is nothing relaxing at all about the game for me. The quote: "A bad day on the golf course is better than a good day in the office" would always come out of someone's mouth and I'd reply, "That is absolutely not correct for me." Many people find golf peaceful and relaxing, I am not one of them.

One of the worse feelings someone can have is regret. We all have decisions that we made or didn't make that we regretted. We've all probably said some things that we wish we could take back. We're human, it's going to happen. What we don't want to have is a "trunk full" of regrets when we are old, replaying our memories in our minds. When you are on your deathbed and the movie of your life replays in your head, are you going to be smiling and happy with all the things you did, or are you going to be unhappy with all the things you didn't do?

I've had older clients share their regrets with me. Some regretted not being around enough when their children were young. Some regretted not taking a job or taking the wrong job. Some thought their life was going to turn out different; how their goals and plans were never met. I've had older clients who traveled and accomplished exactly what they wanted to do in retirement. I've also had bitter and angry clients who were trapped and never realized their dreams.

The way you live your life in retirement is a personal decision for you and your family to reach but know that it is completely in your control. Some folks travel, some start new businesses, some enjoy gardening or woodworking or learn a completely new skill.

Don't wait. Close your eyes and concentrate on what your life movie would be? If you're forty-five years old, statistically, you are halfway through your life. How is the second half of your life going to be different from the first half? At forty-five, many people say, "the first half of my life was growing up and figuring out who I really am, having a family, and getting them off on their own. Now it's my time." So how are you going to live the second half of your life, which is now your time?

You get to direct the second half of your life movie. Is it going to be an adventure movie, a love story, or a boring movie about work, work, and more work?

You've earned this freedom, now what are you going to with it?

CHAPTER NINE

Simplify Your Life

Life should not be a journey to the grave with the intention of arriving safely in a pretty and well preserved body, but rather to skid in broadside in a cloud of smoke, thoroughly used up, totally worn out, and loudly proclaiming, "Wow! What a Ride!"

—Hunter S. Thompson,
The Proud Highway

Retiring early doesn't mean you have to leave the country or uproot and take off to places unknown. Many people are quite content to stay put. Staying put might mean in the house you're currently in, a new home in the same town, or a new home across the state or across the country.

Is It Time to Downsize?

Your last child has just moved out of the house and now you and your spouse live in a 2500+ square-foot home by yourselves. You use one bedroom, kitchen, den, and one bathroom while the rest of the house collects dust. Sure, you're storing all your kid's stuff until they are on their own and can take it off your hands (if they do). Just remember, you're paying the utilities for the whole house while you're only using half the space.

I grew up in a home that was approximately 1600 square feet, which I shared with two adults and two sisters. We used our bedrooms, the two bathrooms, the den, and the kitchen every day. However, the house had a living room and a dining room that went into use only on Thanksgiving and Christmas. This was the "formal" area of the house and, as kids, we were not allowed in those rooms. Combined, those two rooms were probably 300 square feet, so almost 20 percent of the house was, in my eyes, wasted space.

I know this couple, in their early sixties with no children, who built a 10,000-square-foot home. It's just the two of them sitting in a mansion. Why? My first thought was maybe they didn't like each other so they needed the space to hide from each other. My second thought was maybe they wanted to show off how much money they have. Think about how much wasted space is in that house. But with no children and money to burn, they can afford to build what they want and live how they want because they have no heirs to leave it to.

After the kids leave the house, many couples think about downsizing. If you're only using the same four rooms in your house, why not build or move to a smaller home?

Tiny Homes

Turn your TV on to any home improvement channel and you'll see shows on Tiny Homes. According to Small House Society (smallhousesociety.net), a home under 500 square feet is considered a tiny home. This is an area of construction that has exploded over the years due to millennials and baby boomers looking to save on their housing costs. Most Americans spend 1/3 to 1/2 their income putting a roof over their heads, this translates to 15 years of working just to pay for it (per thetinylife.com).

Millennials help drive the tiny home explosion because they're getting out of college with an alarming amount of student loan debt and not wanting to throw money away paying rent or buying a large home with a large mortgage payment. In contrast, baby boomers build tiny homes to cut their costs in retirement and be mortgage free. I recently had a sixty-three-year-old client liquidate her investment, so she could build a tiny home—the condo she owned wasn't going to be paid off for another twenty-five years and she wanted to be mortgage free.

Tiny homes are being built on trailers, so they can be moved to different locales. They are also being built on permanent lots in the middle of the woods, in a field or behind family member homes. That's one of the benefits of a tiny house, you don't need much land to put one on.

Pros and Cons of a Tiny Home

PRO: Low to No Mortgage. If you have the skill set, it's possible to build your own tiny house, saving you thousands of dollars in labor. Often, a tiny home can cost you less than a new car, especially if you already have the land to put it on, so it's quite possible to pay off your home within six or seven years. Just think of the interest you will save by going tiny.

Example: You buy a $250,000 home, finance it for 30 years at a 4 percent interest rate. Over the next 30 years, that $250,000 home is going to cost you a total of $429,674. That's $179,671 in interest paid over the years.

Or: You decide to build a 500-square-foot tiny home, which costs you $50,000. You finance it over a 6-year period at a 4 percent interest rate—you'll pay a little over $16,000 in interest. You'll have it paid within 6 years versus the 30-year treadmill most people get sucked onto.

Back in 2005 and 2006, if you could fog a mirror, you could buy a house and finance it. The government was practically giving away money through Fannie Mae and Ginnie Mae loans. We all know what happened next. In 2008, the housing bubble blew up and millions of people were underwater on their home loans. In the end, people lost their homes due to foreclosures, others gave their homes back to their bank and many sold their homes for steep losses. Most areas of the country have recovered and lending for homes is off and running again. Some of the same parts of the country that overbuilt before now overbuild again. A likely future disaster waiting to happen.

PRO: Less space = less junk = more freedom. Having less than 500 square feet in your home would require you to really downsize your possessions. Think about all the stuff you have that you really don't need anymore. This process really forces you to look at everything in your home and determine what is important to you. Sure, that family heirloom is going in your new home and that antique lamp, but what about all that furniture you bought ten years ago at the local furniture store? Is there any value in taking all of that to your new home? Probably not.

People have become attached to their "stuff" and that stuff can control them if they're not careful. I look at a couch and I see a couch that is something to sit on. However, for some people, that couch might be an heirloom or something precious to them. I look around my home and, besides the photos of my children, their school artwork throughout the years, and videos of them when they were young, most everything in my home is replaceable. My furniture is just something to sit on and I care very little about it. For some people, their home is like a museum where every piece of furniture and decoration has a story, so asking them to downsize might be difficult.

When you de-clutter, you have a sense of freedom. If you live your life with only the things you really need you become free of your possessions.

If you do get rid of furniture and the items that have memories attached to them, you won't lose your memories, they'll just be stimulated a little less frequently. You'll still be able to think about your beloved grandmother and will do so from time to time, even without that entire room full of her heirlooms. Or maybe those memory stimulants are so important that you can't bear to part with them. That makes sense, too.

CON: Less than 500 square feet is small. I remember thinking, "There is no way I could live in five hundred square feet since I'm six-six and closer to three hundred pounds than I am to two hundred pounds." Then I bought an RV and one of the first things I said was, "I could live in this." I'm guessing there is about 200 square feet in my RV, but my thoughts are that in a RV, you spend a good bit of your time outside—which you would probably do with a tiny home as well.

> **SELL IT!**
> Look into your local flea market. One couple I know is starting to downsize now that their daughter is married and living elsewhere. They own a four bedroom-three bath home at 3100 square feet, and every room, including the basement and garage, is filled with "stuff." For the past three months, they pick one Saturday and load some "stuff" into their Toyota pickup and rent a table (or two) at the local flea market. So far, they've made $1100 and it only cost them three Saturday mornings and $60 in table rent. The extra cash goes into their travel fund, and they're looking forward to selling their mammoth house and moving into something smaller one day.
> What "stuff" can you sell to fund some freedom?

Five hundred square feet or less might be perfect for one person, but once you start moving in yourself, your spouse, a child, a dog, and a cat, it might get a little tight. My advice is to visit model units of tiny homes before you decide to buy or build one. On TV, a 350-square-foot home might look quite inviting but 350 square feet is going to feel a lot different when you stand in the middle of it. Make sure this is how you want to live going forward before you commit to owning one.

When I go to Home Depot or Lowe's, I often look at the buildings they have sitting in the parking lot that are normally used for storage. Some of those buildings are quite large and I'm pretty sure I could live in one. All you'd need to do is run electricity, set up the plumbing, add some insulation and drywall and, *bam!*, you have yourself a home.

It's funny, when I was in my twenties I was drawn to owning a

TRY IT TINY
Are you thinking TINY? Why not rent a Tiny Home? Here is just a small sample of places that rent or sell Tiny Homes.

- www.TryItTiny.com
- www.TinyHouseFinder.net
- TinyHouseFor.us
- TinyHouseListings.com

big house in the nicest neighborhood. Now I'm pulling up to Home Depot and spotting a two-story storage building and saying, "Hey, I can live in that." It's interesting how your views change the older you get.

Small Homes

According to the U.S. Department of Housing in 2015, the average size home is now 2687 square feet. That is 1000 square feet more than in 1973. The definition of a tiny home is one that is under 500 square feet and a small home generally ranges from 500 square feet to 1200 square feet.

Not everyone is going to fall in love with a tiny home, but a small home is something that most anyone can fit into their lifestyle. If you think about it, a small home is going to give you a kitchen, den, bathrooms, and bedrooms, so it allows for more separation.

Downsizing to a smaller home can give you flexibility and freedom to do the other things you want to do. For example, you sell your home for $350,000 and buy/build a small home for $150,000. You've just freed up $200,000 to fund other parts of your early retirement. That money could be used for travel or to supplement your income.

Both tiny and small homes accomplish the same things. Both will cut your expenses, potentially allowing you to live mortgage free, or at least save a good bit of money on your mortgage. Both will give you freedom from your possessions and allow you to spend your money funding your adventures.

Whether you go tiny or small is truly a personal decision. What fits your lifestyle best and what you can afford is really what you should be asking yourself.

Off-Grid Living

Off-grid living is the ability to live in a self-sufficient manner without relying on public utilities. When you live off-grid, you get your power from either solar, wind, or a generator. Your water will come from a well or perhaps a fresh water source nearby. Sewage will flow to a septic tank that you'll need to install unless you are living very remote, and then you might find yourself using an outhouse. Normally your food will be raised, such as chickens, or grown in the garden. It's a very simple way of life, but it requires a lot of work.

> ### RESELLING YOUR TINY HOME
> Say you build yourself a tiny home and you want to sell it a few years down the road. Keep in mind, not everyone has the same view of your charming little cottage in the woods that you have. Although tiny homes are very hot these days, at some point this movement might slow down. Many, if not most, homebuyers are still searching for that traditional home, so your tiny home is going to require that special buyer who is looking to downsize. In certain areas of the country, it might be very easy to sell your home, whereas in other areas, it could take some time. For example, here in Asheville, NC, tiny homes sell extremely fast. So, you may or may not have trouble selling it, just be prepared either way.

Off-grid living offers freedom because, after the initial costs of building your homestead, you can save a tremendous amount of money. Most off-grid homes are paid for with cash, so you'll have no mortgage. You'll also have no utility bills so that is quite the savings, and you're growing or raising most of your food supply.

This way of life fascinates me because of the freedom it affords. As a child, I loved the show *Little House on the Prairie*. It wasn't necessarily because of any character on the show or the storylines, but just the uncomplicated way people lived their lives back in the late 1800s. These days, it seems everyone lives such a fast-paced life, barely stopping to slow down to enjoy the moment.

Remember the days prior to cell phones, answering machines, and voicemails? You might if you're old enough. I enjoyed those times when the only way a person could reach you was either by coming by your house or calling your home phone. These days people can

If you are interested in learning more about living a self-sufficient, off-grid lifestyle, check out the following YouTube channels:

- The Boss of the Swamp https://www.youtube.com/user/thebossoftheswamp
- Wranglerstar https://www.youtube.com/user/wranglerstar
- Pure Living for Life https://www.youtube.com/results?search_query=pure+living+for+life

All three offer helpful tips on how to live off-grid.

reach you by cell phone, text, email, voicemail, Facebook, Snapchat, Twitter, FaceTime, Skype, and so on.

Off-grid living is simple living at its best. As simple as it sounds, the one difficulty with living this lifestyle is finding a place where you can do it. You would think that if it's your land, you'd be able to build what you wanted to build, whether that's an off-grid cabin or tiny house or even an off-grid home made from storage containers—especially if you live in a rural area. However, there are many states, counties, and towns that will not allow a home to be built unless it's hooked up to public utilities. Through zoning or some other law, many areas will make you hook up to utilities. The state of Florida, for example, does not allow you to live in a house that is not hooked up to municipal electricity or water. So, finding a spot to build your homestead might be the most difficult part of the equation.

Stay in Your Current Home

By no means am I saying you should downsize or move when you retire early. Often by downsizing, you have more financial flexibility, but it's not something you must do. Let's face it, your home is where you feel most comfortable and where you lay your head at night albeit an RV, a boat, or the house you've owned for the last twenty years. The old saying, "Home is where the heart is," is never truer when you are planning out your adventures in retirement and trying to determine where that "home" might be.

You've lived in the same house for the last twenty-five years. Your children's rooms still have the pencil marks on the wall measuring their height. There is still a hole in the wall in the garage that was never fixed and nobody takes ownership of. Your house has leaks, squeaks, breaks, holes, and other random fixes that no one else knows about. It's your home where you have made lifetime memories.

So, when it comes down to selling your home, whether you sell it to downsize or sell it when you are in your eighties, many people make one mistake. As noted before, they mistake that the memories of their home are based inside the home itself when the memories are based inside themselves and they take those memories with them.

In my home, I do have the pencil marks where I measured my children's height on the door trim. Before I sell, I'll take that door trim off and replace it, so I can take it with me and put it in storage. One other item I will take with me is a large square on the kitchen wall with chalk paint on it. Chalk paint can be sprayed on the wall to make it into a chalkboard. I used an old large picture frame to frame the chalk paint, so it looks like a framed picture. My children, around eight and ten years old, wrote *I love you Dad* and other sayings on the chalk. Before I leave this house, I'll cut that from the wall and take it with me. Besides those two items, my house is just a house, because I'll take all the other great memories with me wherever I go.

My Home Is Paid For

If your home is paid off that changes things a bit. If you have the assets to retire early and you don't need to downsize your home to free up money, then you are in decent shape. The key to retiring early is to have financial freedom and flexibility to do what you want, when you want. So, if your home is paid for, then it's lifted some of burden that might have been anchoring you down financially.

Let's talk about being anchored down. Being anchored down is like having a weight on your shoulders that once lifted leaves you lighter and allows you more freedom. When your mortgage is paid off, you'll still have some costs associated with living in your home. Taxes, utility bills, and the general upkeep of your home can still feel like an anchor, but one that is much easier to digest when you no longer have the mortgage payment.

However, your home could also be anchoring you down mentally. There are spouses who have what I call a split agenda. You might even be in one of these. A split agenda is when you have one spouse who is ready to hit the road traveling and seeking out adventure whereas the other spouse has no desire to do so.

Some people are most comfortable within a ten-mile range of their home. They go to the same gas station to fill up. They go to the same store to buy clothes, and they meet the same people for coffee every Wednesday morning. Basically, they are most comfortable with the same routine. They have created this world of comfort by doing what is predictable. They are anchored in one spot, because they have allowed their mind to be fixated to what is safe. Some people are passionate about the predictability of their routine.

Now this can cause quite the strife in a relationship. You have one spouse ready to travel and the other one not budging on leaving the county that they live in. I have a friend of mine who lost her husband last year. They were high school sweethearts and had been married for almost fifty years. Once he passed away, she started traveling. She told me that her husband was never into traveling and she respected that, but she always had the desire to get out and see the world. She misses her husband dearly but now she is free to travel.

A New Home

Let's say you and your spouse retire early and the only real reason you live in the area you live in is because of your jobs. Now they're a world of opportunities, including moving to the exact area you've always wanted to live. A lot of people will feel a pull to a certain location. Perhaps you are a beach person and you are pulled to live near the ocean. For others, it might be the mountains or a drier climate like Arizona.

As an advisor, I see this quite often with clients. Many would have their primary home in Florida and a vacation home in the mountains of NC. Once they retired, they might go back and forth for a few years, but many ended up selling their Florida home to move to the mountains because that is where they were being pulled to live. Plus, it seemed like every hurricane that came through Florida pushed many to say, "I'm done with this," and move to the mountains.

The options of places to move is unlimited. You may find yourself down to two or three locations that you love, so who's to say that you couldn't try all three to figure out what is best for you. You can always get a storage unit and put the bulk of your possessions in it and just travel with what you really need. Go rent an apartment for six months in each of the locations until you decide what location you love the best.

I've utilized different marketing over my nearly twenty-five years in this industry. A few years ago, I decided to sponsor events at two local high-end apartment communities. It was a very enlightening experience for me to speak to many of the folks who rented these apartments, because what I found were a group of people perfectly content on living in an apartment versus owning a home. Most said they fell in love with Asheville when they traveled here and decided to go home, uproot, and move to Asheville. I asked them if they were renting until they figured out where they wanted to buy. The large

ADVANTAGES OF RENTING YOUR HOME
1. Renting gives you freedom to move about without being tied down to a mortgage. Every six months or year, you can change your location.
2. No yard work or maintenance, because the landlord or rental complex will take care of these items.
3. You can take the money that you would be using as a down payment on a home and invest it.
4. You can afford to live in an area that you might not be able to buy a home in.

majority said no, they planned on living in their apartment with no desire to buy or build a house. As I went further in conversation, I found that most were happy they didn't have to cut their grass and take care of their lawn, or, if something broke in their apartment, all they had to do was call the office and someone came over and fixed it, usually the same day. One person told me that he "banked" the money he made off selling his home up north, which freed up a large amount of money for him to travel. So, don't feel you have to own a house to retire. Renting is just fine and has many advantages.

Action Plan
Life is short, and your freedom is within reach. Don't grow old saying I wish I would have done this or I wish I would have done that. Go do it and never look back. Get your ride started…

✓ Think about how much space you really need.
✓ What "stuff" can you get rid of?
✓ Research alternative homes, rent or buy?

…and simplify your life.

CHAPTER TEN

Mobile Lifestyles

Wealth is the ability to fully experience life.

—Henry David Thoreau

Whether by land or by sea, retiring early affords you the freedom to travel. If you are enticed to travel on land and see the National Parks and visit areas that you've never seen before, then a recreational vehicle (RV) might be just what you need. However, some folks have a passion for water and the open seas, so they opt to buy a boat to live on. We will explore both in this chapter.

Recreational Vehicles

Since the advent of the covered wagon in 1745, people have traveled the land using their wagons as a living space. In the 1800s, circus performers used motor vehicles or trailers equipped with a living space. By the 1920s, these traveling trailers came equipped with many amenities found in homes, such as kitchens and baths, and were used mostly for camping and family vacations.

Today, more RVs occupy the roads, with new RVs rolling off the lots in record numbers and used RVs advertised everywhere. Two thousand sixteen was a record year for the RV industry and 2017 is possibly going to be better than 2016.

So why are RVs so popular right now? Cost is one attraction. There is an RV for everyone's budget from the low end "Cousin Eddie" used RV to a $2 million luxury Motorhome. There are new travel trailers and fifth-wheel RVs that can be bought for less than a new F150 pickup and used motorhomes that can be bought for less than a 5-year-old Honda Sedan.

I've also spoken to a few folks who say RVing is easier than flying these days. It seems that going through security at major airports has worn some people out, so they prefer to drive to their destination. (Visit www.rvia.org/?ESID=indicators for other factors that contribute to RV growth.)

Full-Time RVing

A growing number of folks are selling nearly every possession they have and jumping into their RV and taking off full time. It's not just the sixty-five-year-old retirees who are doing it. Individuals and couples under fifty years old are a rapidly growing group in the RV community. It's common to see young families with small children traveling full time.

What better way to educate your children on the Grand Canyon than to travel there and show it to them. Just think of the memories you will make if you tour the United States, seeing all the places you've heard about but have never seen. How about taking a trip up to Canada and continuing to Alaska? These are memories that you'll never forget.

I know people right now who have never been out of the state of North Carolina, never once been on an airplane or really left their home town. The reason? Mostly excuses: I don't have the money, I can't take time off from work, I can't leave my family, or perhaps fear has just set in. So not everyone will be ready for a mobile lifestyle.

About a year and a half ago, I stumbled on to a YouTube video hosted by Bob Wells of CheapRVLiving.com that changed my life forever. Watching one video turned into two then three and, next I knew, it was like I was binge-watching *Breaking Bad*. Wells's videos were interviews with people who had left their jobs and hit the road full time. Some folks were on the road in vans and travel trailers and each of them had fascinating stories. I was hooked, and I had to find out more about this nomad lifestyle.

I quickly found other YouTubers who were on the road full time, such as Steve and Courtney from "A Streamin Life," Ben and Rebecca from "His and Hers Alaska," Jaime from "Enigmatic Nomadics," Howie from "Howie Roll," and many others who helped shape my thoughts and ideas of full-time RVing. I fell in love with the idea of owning an RV and traveling the country.

I spent about eight months searching for the perfect RV. I wanted a big RV. No, I wanted a small RV. I wanted a fifth-wheel. No, I wanted a 40-foot diesel pusher. I went to RV shows, dealerships, and watched hours upon hours of videos of reviews of various RVs. Quite simply, I became overloaded with information. I ended up buying a nine-year-old Holiday Rambler 31-foot Class A motorhome mainly because I didn't have to duck walk through it, and I could stand in the shower.

RVs come in varied sizes from a 45-foot Class A motorhome to a regular size Class B van. You might have anywhere from 50 square feet to 350 square feet depending on the size you get.

Here are the differences:

Travel Trailers are towable and can be pulled with a truck, SUV, or potentially a car, depending on the size. They can range from 12 feet to 35 feet.

Pros:
- Your current vehicle might be able to tow a travel trailer, so it may not require you to purchase another vehicle.

- Easy to pull and set up.
- The price for a new travel trailer will range between $11,000 to $35,000. The average cost being $23,000.

Cons:
- You may have to purchase another vehicle to pull it.
- Be careful of the quality. Not all, but many of the travel trailers have lower-end quality.

Fifth Wheel is a towable RV pulled by a truck that has a special hitch in the center of its bed. The length of a fifth wheel can be anywhere from 22 feet to over 40 feet. These typically have two levels for living space and sleeping space. Why is it called a fifth wheel? The term originally comes from horse drawn carriages back in the mid-1800s. The fifth-wheel coupling system allowed the front axle to pivot to better assist in turning.

Pros:
- Fifth wheels can be very spacious and can give you more interior room than any other RV.
- Generally, they have better overall quality than a travel trailer.
- The price for a new fifth wheel will range between $15,000 to over $100,000. The average cost is around $40,000.

Cons:
- You'll have to buy a pickup truck to pull it, if you don't already have one, which could cost you another $25,000 to $70,000 after you purchase a fifth wheel.
- With the larger fifth wheels, you may not be able to park in every RV, National, or State park.

Class A Motorhomes are motorized RVs, built on a heavy-duty chassis that can range from 21 feet to 45 feet. Couples who do a lot of traveling will often pull a tow vehicle with their Class A Motorhome so that when they reach their destination, they have a separate vehicle they can travel around in.

Pros:
- The unit is self-contained, so you are not pulling it with a truck or SUV.
- The larger Class As are like a rolling condominium, which offer plenty of living space and storage.
- The price for a new Class A will range between $75,000 to over $1,000,000. The average cost is $100,000.

Cons:
- Gas mileage is going to be between 7 mpg to 10 mpg.
- Most likely, you'll need a tow vehicle to pull with the motorhome so when you park it, you'll have a way to get around.

Class B Motorhomes are the smallest motorized RVs that are quickly becoming the most popular motorhomes. Their popularity comes from them having the best gas mileage of all the motorhomes, and they generally can be parked in a regular parking space. This makes them perfect for individuals or couples who don't want the hassle of towing another vehicle.

Pros:
- Easier to drive, as it's not much bigger than a regular SUV or truck. The length is generally between 16 to 24 feet.
- Gas mileage can range from 15 mpg to 22 mpg.
- The price for a new Class B will range between $40,000 to $150,000. The average cost is $75,000.

Cons:
- You'll have limited living and storage space.
- Interior height could be an issue for some. (You may not be able to stand up inside it.)

Class C Motorhomes can be thought of as a mix between a class A and a class B. They are typically not as large as a class A but not as small as a class B. Generally, a Class C Motorhome will have an over-the-cab sleep area and will typically have a 28-foot maximum length.

Pros:
- Can generally sleep 4–6 adults and kids.
- Easier to drive than a Class A but not quite as maneuverable as a Class B.
- The price for a new Class C will range between $50,000 to $250,000. The average cost is $70,000.

Cons:
- Gas mileage is poor. Class Cs generally get between 8 mpg to 12 mpg.
- Storage is better than a Class B but not quite as good as a Class A.

Truck Camper is a camper shell that attaches to the back of your truck. They generally range between 8 feet to almost 12 feet in length. There have been huge improvements with truck campers over the years with many having toilets, showers, kitchens, and expanded living spaces.

Pros:
- If you have a four-wheel-drive truck with a camper attached, it allows you to go deeper into the backcountry than most RVs.
- The camper can be easily attached to your truck and removed.
- The price for a new truck camper will range between $3000 to $65,000. The average cost is $25,000.

Cons:
- Smaller living space.
- You may have to buy a truck or, if you already own a truck, you may have to get a larger one depending on the size of the camper.

Miscellaneous: Some folks are converting cargo vans, school buses, old Greyhound buses, step vans, military vehicles, and cargo trailers into campers. You're only limited by your imagination.

Every RV/Motorhome has positives and negatives, so it really depends on how you plan on using it. For our purposes, we are going to look at using your RV as a full-time home.

Should I Buy a New or Used RV?

It really depends on you and what you are looking for. If you are the type of person who needs the security of a warranty and wants the newest bells and whistles, then buying new is probably for you. However, you're often going to find better deals on used models. Many used RVs are like that new $1000 treadmill that people buy—use it a few times a year and then slowly never use it again. So, it's possible to find RVs that are ten years old, in great shape, with low miles, and at very reasonable prices.

Just because you buy new, don't expect everything to be perfect with your RV—this is a common myth that many people fall for. Many times, people buy new RVs because they think, "It's new so it's not going to have someone else's problems." There are often problems and bugs to work out on brand new RVs and, yes, the warranty will take care of most of those problems, but just don't assume that since it's new, it's not going to have issues.

When I was looking for my motorhome, I had a pretty good idea of what I wanted, but I was still confused on where I was going to find it. One website that was helpful for me was www.pplmotorhomes. com—an RV dealership in Houston that has the floorplans of every

RV they have listed for sale. Now, I bought my RV from a private party but seeing different floorplans on their site allowed me to eliminate many RVs I had considered.

When buying an RV, my advice is to consider the lifestyle you want. This will help you figure out the type and size of RV you'll need. If you are going to live in it full time, consider how much space you'll need. Are you going to try and move your home into your RV, or do you plan on taking a minimal amount and selling the rest of your possessions? Everyone is different, so buy what fits your own budget, needs, and requirements.

Where to Camp for Free

If you plan on traveling North America and staying in RV parks along the way, then any RV/Motorhome is going to work for you. However, where you really save money is when you can "Boondock." Boondocking, also known as dry camping, is where you park somewhere and are not hooked up to electricity, water, or sewage. Typically, RVers who are boondocking are staying in a Wal-Mart, Cracker Barrel, or Cabela's parking lots as well as rest stops, casinos, or on public lands.

You might question the thought of staying in a Wal-Mart or Cracker Barrel parking lot. Most RVers use these as a place to park for the night as they are passing through the area. Think about this: you are crossing the country and it's going to take you four days to do so. You'll probably be driving six to ten hours a day so when you're tired and are just ready to grab some dinner and go to bed, a Wal-Mart parking lot is going to be an attractive spot. Otherwise, you'll be looking around for a campground to stay at for twelve hours before hitting the road again.

Bureau of Land Management (BLM)

In the western part of the United States, millions of acres spread out over multiple states that are managed by the Bureau of Land

Management (BLM). BLM land is free to camp on for up to fourteen days. After fourteen days, you can move on to another BLM site. So, you can camp year-round if you wanted to and not pay a dime in RV park fees or rent (see www.blm.gov/visit for places to explore). National and State Parks, the U.S. Forest Service, and County Parks are also options, but there could be a small fee attached to camp in these areas.

If you want to live rent free, you could go to Arizona, Colorado, Montana, Utah, Wyoming, Idaho, Nevada, and many other states and live free in your RV/Motorhome on BLM land. BLM also has areas that they deem Long Term Visitor Areas that you don't have to move every fourteen days, but there is a fee if you decide to stay in one area for the winter or summer months.

BLM land tends to be in the desert or areas that have higher altitudes. It's land that would be otherwise unuseable except for grazing animals. What I find great about BLM land is that you can be near other RVers and campers if you'd like or be in complete isolation.

So, if your goal is to camp on BLM much of time, then your choice of RV/Motorhome is very important. A lot of BLM land can be reached just right off the highway, but much of it is down miles and miles of dirt roads. Some are maintained well, and some are not. So, if you go out and buy that 45-foot Class A rolling condo expecting to live on BLM land year-round, you can do it, but you'll be limited to where you can go. I can't imagine you'll try driving it three miles down a dirt road in the middle of the desert.

If your plan is to go deep into the desert and wilderness, then a truck camper that is four-wheel drive, or a Class B that has front-wheel drive, might be your best bet. At the end of the day, the bigger motorhomes are going to give you more room and luxuries, but you are not going to have the freedom to go anywhere you like. The smaller RVs/Motorhomes are going to give you more freedom to travel in and out of where you want to go, but you are going to sacrifice space.

One way or another, you are going to sacrifice something, so it really boils down to what is more important to you.

How to Make Money on the Road

If your plan is to retire early and hit the road, you may need to work along the way. Here is a list of jobs, which are common for folks who travel the country in their RVs.

Camp Host: As a camp host, you could be expected to collect fees, work in an office checking people in, work maintaining the campground or park, and help the other campers. You'll be working in exchange for a free campsite and, in some cases, a small compensation. Camp hosting jobs are usually available between May and September each year and year-round in the warmer states.

Digital Nomad: Whether it's designing websites, writing a blog, having a YouTube channel, offering up your social media skills, plenty of ways exist to make money online and on the road. All you need is a computer and an Internet connection and you're in business.

Sugar Beet Harvest: The Sugar Beet Harvest is a short-term job that lasts only three to four weeks, generally beginning at the end of September and ending in October. It's a popular job among RVers because it pays well for just a few short weeks and if you are in good health, you can do this job. The locations of these jobs are in Montana, North Dakota, and Minnesota. (See www.sugarbeetharvest.com/ for more information.)

Amazon: Amazon loves RVers and, in fact, they have given them a name. Amazon CamperForce (http://www.workamper.com/femp/153589/index.html) offers RVers the ability to work at an Amazon distribution center for the last three or four months of the year. You'll get a free campsite and you'll be paid for your time, plus the ability to get overtime at time and a half. Much like the Sugar Beet Harvest, this isn't backbreaking work. Generally, you can expect to be packing and shipping goods for the holiday season.

Gate-Guarding at Oil Fields: These jobs are mostly located in Texas. The job is working the gate at an oil field. You would be responsible for checking people in and out of the gate and general security for the area. Most gate-guarding jobs prefer couples with RVs with experience as ex-police or ex-military, but that's not always the case. The hours are long, and the spots can be very remote, but it can be a stable source of income.

RV Tech: What better way to earn money, surrounded by other RVers, than to be able to offer up your services as a mechanic?

Traveling Nurses: If you're a nurse by trade, there is great money to be made as a traveling nurse. You'll be able to pick which parts of the country that you wish to work and be on your way to a different destination before too long.

Construction Workers: Construction workers are always in demand across the country especially if you have a specific skill set.

Seasonal Jobs: Ski resorts, Christmas tree farms, amusement parks, and local tourist shops can be wonderful places to get temporary work.

Bartending: If you're a bartender by trade, you should be able to find a job in pretty much any medium-size to larger city.

Casino Dealer: Being a trained poker or blackjack dealer can afford you the luxury of traveling across the country and finding gainful employment at pretty much any casino. There are dealers who travel the country and are hired on when there is big demand, such as when the World Series of Poker comes to a casino.

I've just scratched the surface on the jobs that are available on the road. The great part is you can work all year, half the year, or just a few months. It all depends on your income needs and where you want to travel.

It's also possible to take your current job on the road. Now, this isn't exactly retiring early, but it does give you some control to work where and when you want. I recently spoke to the head of a social media marketing company who mentioned that one of his friends, a

CEO of a tech company, recently sold everything in NYC and took off to travel the country, working out of his Airstream. All he needs is a cell phone, Internet connection, and a scanner and he can work anywhere in the world.

Cost of Full-Time RVing

It could cost you a lot less than your current monthly bills, or it could cost you a lot more. The real key is how you plan on living on the road.

Could a single person live full time on $1000 a month? Absolutely. If your RV is paid for, you stay primarily on BLM land or boondock year-round, and you cook your meals versus eating out every night, then $1000 or less is very possible. One of the costliest expenses is gas/diesel. If you are mostly staying put in a general area, then gas isn't going to be a major expense for you. However, if you are jumping from state to state and always on the move, then keeping your budget under $1000 will be difficult.

As a couple, $1000 a month might be tight, but it is doable if you budget your expenses and stay strict in your spending habits. A more reasonable budget for a couple is $2500 a month.

However, if you still have an RV payment *and* you must stay at a campground every night *and* you eat out at restaurants seven nights a week, then it's possible that your budget might be $4000 or more each month.

RVing can get very expensive if you're not careful. If you plan to live full time in your RV, it is extremely important to budget your expenses and have a game plan before taking off on the road. Be sure to set aside an emergency fund for unexpected expenses; much like your brick and mortar home repairs, maintenance will always need to be done.

Crunching the Numbers

Let's say you develop a budget and find that you'll need $2300 a month for both you and your spouse to be able to retire early and take off in your RV full time. The problem is when you find out that the income you have coming in is only $1800 a month. You have a $500 a month shortfall or income gap. How do you make it work?

You could make up the difference with your savings but that's tricky because you want to make sure you have enough as an emergency fund. I wouldn't suggest this unless you have a large savings.

The better way would be to get one of the jobs I mentioned earlier and work for two or three months to make up the shortfall. Let's say you worked as a camp host in Yellowstone National Park for a few months. It's possible that both you and your spouse would make enough to cover your shortfall. There is nothing wrong with working a few months in a beautiful part of the country and having the other months completely free to go and do whatever you please.

Ideally, you'd want to be in a position that if your expenses are $2300 a month, you have $3000 or more of income coming in. If the shortfall isn't too large, it can be overcome by working as you travel.

Traveling Alone

Not all people traveling around the country are couples. A growing number of single women and single men travel the country in their RVs/vans. You might think being a single traveler that you would get lonely. It's only lonely if you want to be lonely.

Large networks of traveling singles exist that organize events and rallies all over the country. Often a group of single RVers will caravan together into Mexico, Canada, Alaska, and across the United States together. These networks can be found on Facebook and websites such as Loners on Wheels (www.lonersonwheels.com) and Escapees (www.escapees.com). What is nice about these groups is that you can be as involved as you want to be. So, if you want to go off on your own for stretches and then gather back with a group of like-minded singles, you can certainly do so.

RVers are an exceptional group of people. I've heard of many lifelong friendships made on the road. If you live in a neighborhood, how many of your neighbors do you truly know? Often, people come home from work, drive right into their garage, and go inside of their home not to be seen again until they leave for work the next day. With a group of RVers, it's a community that really watches out for one another. Whether it's sitting by a campfire as a group or meeting up at an organized gathering, you'll have the opportunity to bond with like-minded people.

Safety on the Road

Much like your travels in everyday life, it pays to be aware of your surroundings. It's no different when you're full-time RVing.

It's very common for RVers to bring along their pets on the road with them. Having a dog that barks at every sound outside of your RV is not a terrible thing, especially if you're camping out in a remote area. Be aware that many RV parks do not allow aggressive breed dogs into their parks, but if you are on BLM land or boondocking, you should be fine. I have a 185-pound English Mastiff named Zeus. Zeus looks menacing, but he is a big baby and wouldn't hurt a fly, but he would not be allowed into many RV parks because of his breed.

Many RVers have guns to protect themselves. It's best to check with each state that you'll be traveling in to see what that state's specific laws are. A state like California is much stricter on guns than a state like Alabama, so it's best to know what those laws are before traveling through.

If you plan on going to Mexico in your RV, DO NOT TAKE YOUR GUNS INTO MEXICO. Please get a storage locker and store your guns before entering the country. Mexico has very strict gun laws and I doubt you want to spend a few years in a Mexican prison.

If you plan on going to Alaska, you can register your guns at the Canadian border and they will allow you to pass through Canada to Alaska. Be sure to look up the guidelines prior to your trip because they can change.

Full-Time RVing. Is It for You?

Selling everything you own and jumping into your RV to live in full time is not for everyone. But for many people it checks all the boxes they are looking for when they retire

PEACE OF MIND
Not sure yet if you're ready to buy an RV, why not rent one? RVshare.com allows you to book any class of RV throughout the United States, and they have 24-hour travel concierge and roadside assistance. Sign up for their free magazine or check out their blog. How's that for peace of mind?

early. Hitting the road can be peaceful, less stress than your everyday life, less expensive than your old life and when you're ready to change your neighborhood, you turn the key and move on down the road.

Most people never come close to seeing a sizable portion of the United States. Why not change that? Make a list of the places you want to go see in the United States and then go see them.

Full-Time Boating

Over my lifetime, I've met some boat fanatics and they were passionate about being on the water whenever they could. It was almost like they were at peace the most in their life when they were on the water.

Having a boat on which you can live is very freeing because you could set sail and go to Bermuda, the Caribbean, the Great Lakes, or sail around the world if that is a goal for you. Much like full-time RVing, you can change your neighborhood when you so desire.

What Type of Boating Will You Do?

Before you buy, you want to make sure you have a clearly defined plan for how you want to use the boat. Some folks want to cruise the Caribbean whereas other might never leave the intracoastal waterway on the East Coast. Heck, I've read that they're people who buy boats to live on and never leave the harbor. Whatever floats your boat.

Knowing how you plan on using your boat will help you determine what size boat you will need.

Sailboats, such as a single hull or catamarans, which have two hulls, work great for full-time living. A catamaran will have much more space than a single hull (mono-hulled) boat, so if you need as much space as possible on your sail boat, a catamaran might be your best bet. If space isn't a concern, a single-hulled sailboat might be best for an individual or a couple.

Pros:
- Less fuel costs, because you can use wind power sailing versus fuel for your motor. However, you will have the option to use the motor if there is no wind.
- Catamarans are generally more stable to sail.
- Catamarans can also carry multiple passengers and have a lot of space.

Cons:
- Rigging can be arduous work for some and might take multiple people to fully rig a large sailboat.
- Repairs can be costly. Whether it's replacing the sails, engine repair, or other components on a boat, repair costs can quickly add up.

A *powerboat* can give you more room and the ability to travel faster to your destination. However, now you must factor in fuel costs whether it's a gas or a diesel engine.

Pros:
- More stability. A powerboat general sits higher in the water than a sailboat does, which gives you more comfort if you decide to live on one full time.

- Speed. You get to your destination faster.
- When you get to your boat, you jump on, crank the motor, and get going. No worries about rigging sails.

Cons:
- If you are moving around a good bit, fuel will be expensive.
- Much like sailboats, repair costs can be expensive.
- Maintenance can be expensive.

Houseboats are another option, but these are normally found inland versus in an ocean harbor. If you are looking to hit the ocean, then a houseboat is not an option. If you plan on putting it on a river and living in it full time, then that's where a houseboat is great. For a houseboat, the calmer the water, the better.

Pros:
- Much like a mortgage, the interest that you pay on a houseboat can be tax deductible. As long as it has a toilet, bedroom, and kitchen, it's a tax deduction for you.
- Generally cheaper fuel costs, because houseboats aren't moved around as often as say a powerboat.
- Depending on where you live, you may not have to pay property tax on your houseboat. (Check your local ordinances.)

Cons:
- You may have dock fees as well as home owner association fees.
- It's a boat and much like your brick and mortar house, there will be maintenance and repair costs. Because it's a boat, those costs could be more expensive.
- With all boats, your stability is weather dependent. Just because you're on an inland river or lake doesn't mean that a storm might not roll up and shake you up a bit.

Cost of Full-Time Boating

When you are doing your planning for moving on to a boat, you'll need to consider the lifestyle you'll be living. Do you plan to be docked in a marina most nights where you'll have electricity? If so, then there will be dock fees that you'll have to pay. Dock fees are usually charged by the length of your boat, so the bigger the boat the more expensive it is. Anchoring your boat out in the water can save you a lot of money because you won't have to pay the fees to dock. When you anchor out in the water, you can take your dinghy into the marina. Keep in mind, however, that some marinas will charge you a landing fee for parking your dinghy in the marina, so it might not be totally free when you anchor out.

Gas could be a major expense if you plan on being on the go all the time. However, if you plan on being in one marina for six months and then traveling to another marina for another six months, gas won't be a major expense.

You'll have regular expenses such as clothes, food, cell phone bill, Internet, insurance on the boat, and health insurance as you would regardless of where you live.

Maintenance can end up being the biggest expense if you're not careful. I'm sure you've heard the old saying, "The two happiest days of a boat owner's life is the day they buy it and the day they sell it." The other one I've heard is, "B.O.A.T. which stands for Bring Out Another Thousand." I'd suggest that both sayings apply to the maintenance and upkeep costs that boats have. Therefore, it is so important to do your homework on the front end when you're buying a boat. Hiring a marine surveyor for a few hundred dollars to look over the boat before you buy it can save you thousands of dollars in the future.

Should I Buy a New or Used Boat?

Much like we discussed with buying a new or used RV, just because you buy a new boat, don't expect everything to be perfect on it. However, with a new boat, it will come with a warranty that will fix most of the items. (Be sure to read the fine print on any warranty.)

Buying new or used is really a personal and financial choice. If this is your first boat, then it might be wise to buy used to make sure you are going to enjoy the lifestyle. If you've owned multiple boats and you know that brand new boat is exactly what you want, and it fits your budget, then go for it. Just know, like any other vehicle, be careful of the depreciation. In the boating world, there is a boat for pretty much anyone's budget.

Working from a Boat

If you're docked in a harbor, then working from a boat is no different than working from a house. You'd be able to commute back and forth to a job. However, if you're on the water 90 percent of the time then it's a bit different. If you have an Internet connection, being a digital nomad is a trendy way to make money on the water. Setting up websites, consulting, or blogging about your travels are all great ways to make money on the water.

Ideally, you've retired early and don't have to work. There are people who will take off for the Caribbean or Mexico for months at a time only to return for a few months to work, save up, and take off again. Everyone does it differently so make your plan customized to you.

Safety

Watch out for pirates. (I'm kidding, sort of.) If you plan on boating through international waters, you do want to be aware of any warnings that have been issued. You'll want to do your homework before bringing a firearm along with you. Having a shotgun onboard while you move up and down the intracoastal waterway is one thing. Going into a Mexican harbor with a loaded shotgun is completely different. Research the laws or there could be major ramifications if you make a wrong decision here.

Full-Time Boating. Is It for You?

Are you ready to pack up and take off on a boat? It's a dream for many people to sail the high seas or just travel up and down the coastline. Depending on your plan, living on a boat can be much less expensive than your brick and mortar life, or it can be a lot more expensive. Do your homework, have a budget, an emergency fund, and a plan before you set sail. Plot your course and live the dream.

Other Lifestyles

Many people have passions and lifestyles that aren't about traveling the country sleeping in a RV or living on a boat full time. For example, take folks who are passionate about riding motorcycles. Every spring, summer, and fall in Western North Carolina where I live, hordes of motorcyclists travel in and around the mountains. Whether they are in the mountains to ride the Tail of the Dragon (a road that has 318 curves in 11 miles) or just to ride the other mountain roads to enjoy a peaceful getaway, the passion they have is evident. As previously noted, for an avid motorcyclist, August in Sturgis, South Dakota, is like Mecca. Whether you ride a Harley, BMW, Kawasaki, Honda, or Ducati, Sturgis attracts all types of riders—from the Hell's Angel biker to the investment banker biker.

Retiring early and having a mobile lifestyle doesn't always mean you will be selling off every possession and leaving town. Plenty of people are content on always returning to a home base. For many motorcyclists, going out on the weekends and taking shorter trips here and there satisfies their itch to hit the road. For others, it's taking off for longer trips, such as to Sturgis, Myrtle Beach, or Daytona that they are passionate about. Gas costs are generally minimal and adventure prospects maximal.

I had a client who retired at age fifty-eight and had never ridden a motorcycle a day in his life. About three weeks into retirement, he decides to go out and buy a Harley Davidson and not just any Harley, it was one of the big ones. When I met with him after about a month after he bought it, he started telling me stories. The first time he sat on it, it toppled over on him. He then tells me he's riding across a corn field (who rides a Harley across a corn field?) and he dropped the bike again. As he's telling me these things, I can tell he's getting upset at me because I'm laughing. However, a month after getting it, he says that he's almost stress free when he rides and now understands why people love their bikes.

Another mobile lifestyle that people enjoy, and will retire early to do more of, is flying. Having your pilot's license affords you a large amount of freedom and allows you to come and go across the country as you please. What's not to like when you have access to a plane and the ability to take off and fly three hundred miles away for the day or weekend?

Many pilots have their own plane, but there are ways to fly without having your own plane. These days you can rent a plane, or you can join a flying club that will give you access to a plane. Pilots are passionate about their craft and always honing their skills to become a better pilot. It's like its part hobby and part lifestyle. Although I'm best with two feet planted on the ground, having the ability to travel by flying and avoid crowded airports, roads, and marinas must be very liberating. I've spoken with pilots in the past who have told me that they are the most at peace when they are flying. Much like motorcyclists who are generally at peace riding down the road.

What is your passion? Where are you most at peace? Generally, doing the things you enjoy the most and are passionate about will give you the most peace in your life. It's hard to be at peace when you don't have the time to follow your passion. Working sixty to seventy hours a week until you are sixty-five years old is not the solution. Yes, you will have more money, but you will have lost out on valuable time that you'll never get back. So, are you living life or just going through the motions?

Action Plan

Follow your passions. Whether it's RVing, sailing, riding your bike, flying, or perhaps it's something else, here are the four things you need to think about:

- ✓ What kind of mobile lifestyle do you want?
- ✓ What's your living budget?
- ✓ Do you have an emergency fund?
- ✓ Have you planned your travels?

Remember, corporate America will work you into the ground if you allow it. Step up, take back control of your life, and retire as soon as you can.

CHAPTER ELEVEN

Become an Expat

Man is free at the moment he wishes to be.

—Voltaire

What is an expat? Expat is short for expatriate. According to Merriam-Webster, it means to leave one's native country to live elsewhere. So, what makes someone move to a foreign country? The sense of adventure, the different culture, and the passion of traveling are just some of the reasons people choose to take off. Perhaps you married someone from a foreign country and chose to live in their native country instead of yours. But the number one reason, and what we focus on here in this chapter, is the financial savings (cost of living) of moving to a different country.

Financial Savings

In the United States, can you live comfortably on an income of $1500 a month? I'd say most people would answer no. The key is "comfortably." Most people could live on $1500 a month if they strip away the comforts of home. Parts of the United States are more reasonable to reside in than others, however, in the most reasonable areas in the country, how far will $1500 a month take you? Therefore, many Americans are picking up and moving to a foreign country. Their money will stretch farther in a less expensive foreign land.

Fifteen hundred a month will no longer buy you the American dream. Years ago, it could. If your parents are in their sixties and seventies, go ask them what they paid for their first home. I bet they paid more for the last car they bought than they paid for their first home. The cost of living in the United States is increasing every year due to the cost of goods getting more expensive. The cost of food, healthcare, automobiles, utilities, and real estate have all increased over the last ten years and will continue to do so.

Inflation is the costs of goods that appreciate over time. Think back when you were a kid. How much did it cost you to buy a movie ticket, a drink, and popcorn? When I was a kid, I remember I could get all three for about $6. Today, you're looking at $20+ for each person—for a family of four, the idea of going to the movies on the weekend is nearly extinct.

In 2017, the government reported that we had very little inflation, roughly around 2 percent in 2016. I call BS on this number. You see, the number they give us is a skewed number. What is not told is that the formula that calculates inflation (Consumer Price Index) is manipulated—the components of the formula have changed over the years. So really, the formula can be changed to give any number the government wants to give to the public.

At the end of the day, we know it's getting more expensive to live in the United States, which is why more people are looking at alternatives. Where can you live so that the money you earn stretches farther? Mexico, Ecuador, Costa Rica, Panama, Thailand, and Vietnam are a few countries where expats find that their U.S. dollar goes a long way. Countries like Canada, Germany, the UK, Italy, and Japan also have large expat populations, but you'll struggle to find huge financial benefits moving to these more established, developed countries.

Again, the goal for most is to stretch their money and that's hard to do in Germany or England.

So why are Latin America and Southeast Asia such popular destinations? Mostly because the weather is tropical and the cost of living in these areas

CPI—AN UNKNOWN ENTITY
According to Investopedia, the Consumer Price Index is composed of two numbers—one measures only 89 percent of the urban population while the other is a subset that measures only 28 percent of this population. This number does not include nonmetro populations, farm families, armed forces, and people serving in prison and those in mental hospitals. (See https://www.investopedia.com/terms/c/consumer priceindex.asp.)

is much cheaper than the United States. Remember, in the United States, you'll be hard-pressed to live comfortably on an income of $1500 a month. In certain parts of Latin America and Southeast Asia, you can live very comfortably on an income of $1500 a month or less. You'll want to do your homework because many cities and neighborhoods in these areas can cost you as much as you currently pay in the United States.

How can I make money if I live in a foreign country? The Internet does not have borders. An online business would be the most ideal job, but if you don't have that skillset there are other ways. If you move to a country that has a large expat population, you can market to them. You could market to tourists if you are in a large tourist destination. Get a job locally teaching English. In Mexico, there are Wal-Marts, Costco's, Best Buy's, etc., where you could get a job. The key is, if you plan on working, have a plan in place before you arrive.

When doing research for this book, I found that the U.S. State Department does not track the number of people moving out of the United States. They can give you an estimate, based on military personnel stationed around the world and can guess at the number of non-military, but at the end of the day, they have no real idea how many Americans live full time outside the United States. The

IRS might have a better idea of how many Americans file tax returns from outside the United States, but no real number exists from them either. Bottom line, the U.S. government does not actively track expats from around the globe, so it's difficult to define the number of people doing it.

Speaking of the IRS, just because you move to a different country doesn't mean that you're off the hook with Uncle Sam. You must file your tax return just as you would if you live in the United States. The IRS does give you an automatic two-month extension if you live outside the United States, so your tax returns will be due on June 15th instead of April 15th each year. (See www.irs.gov/individuals/in ternational-taxpayers/u-s-citizens-and-resident-aliens-abroad for more information.)

One area that the government does track is the number of people renouncing their U.S. citizenship. Renouncing your U.S. citizenship isn't as easy as emailing your Uncle Sam and telling him that you quit. It's a complicated process that will cost you money and potentially trigger taxes when you decide to leave. (Are you curious about why people may renounce their citizenship, visit www.investopedia. com/articles/personal-finance/060515/why-people-renounce-their-us-citizenship.asp.)

The Foreign Earned Income Exclusion (FEIE), if certain qualifications are met, allows a citizen, living abroad, to exclude up to $102,100 in income for 2017 (www.irs.gov). So, if you are making $102,100 and qualify for the FEIE, you will pay zero in federal taxes to the IRS. Let's say you are making $150,000, then you'll be subject to pay taxes on $47,900 ($150,000 − $102,100 = $47,900). You also may be able to deduct certain housing costs as well.

Keep in mind, if you are living in a foreign country and have started a business in that country, you'll be subject to that country's income tax. It would be best to hire an accountant versed in international taxation if you do decide to open a business abroad.

Which Countries Are Americans Moving to?

It should be no surprise that Canada, Mexico, and most of Central America comprise the largest number of U.S. expats. The United Kingdom, Philippines, Italy, Japan, and Germany are also popular destinations overseas. It's estimated that Mexico has over one million Americans living there.

The following six countries are extremely popular with expats due to the lower cost of living, culture, weather, and so on.

Mexico

Why is Mexico attractive financially? It's because the cost of living is much cheaper in Mexico than in the United States. Now, if you are determined to live a big lifestyle in Mexico, you can spend as much or even more than what you spend in the United States. However, most people move to Mexico to save money.

For example, take Mérida, a city with over 750,000 residents that has all the luxuries of a large U.S. city.

- Rent 3-bedroom apartment in the city, $400 a month
- Internet, $25 a month
- Meal for 2 at a medium range restaurant, $20
- Domestic bottled Beer, $1.40
- Basic Utilities (electric, water, gas, etc.), $70 a month

SHOULD YOU RENOUNCE YOUR U.S. CITIZENSHIP?

Renouncing your U.S. citizenship is possible but not suggested as you will lose your rights as a citizen of the United States. According to *The Telegraph*, 5,411 Americans renounced their citizenship in 2016, which was 26 percent more than in 2015. The United States requires Americans living in foreign countries to report financial information on bank and investment accounts held in countries outside the United States, which is a big reason why people who do not plan on moving back to the states, will renounce their citizenship.

The process of renouncing your citizenship is time-consuming and expensive. I do not advocate for dropping U.S. Citizenship, but if you have a pressing need I would only suggest you do all your homework and research the process and what it means.

Depending on where you look in Mexico, some cities are going to be more or less expensive than Mérida.

Healthcare is another reason folks move to Mexico or at least cross the border for treatment. I've had a couple of clients over the years fly into El Paso and then go into Mexico to get dental work done. They told me they saved 70 percent on their dental work in Mexico versus their U.S. dentists. I asked them if they were concerned about the service they got and they both said that their dentist went to U.S. dental schools and they felt very satisfied with the work. One of the clients has returned to Mexico multiple times for treatments.

There are several ways you can pay for your healthcare in Mexico. Paying out of pocket is popular because of the reasonable costs of basic treatment. If you're working in Mexico, you should have access to the Instituto Mexicano del Seguro Social (IMSS), which is a national system that is free for the participant. Not everyone will qualify for the IMSS due to eligibility

Pharmaceutical prices, in general, are also a lot cheaper in Mexico than in the United States. Matter of fact, many drugs that require a prescription in the United States do not require a prescription in Mexico. Antibiotics are one such drug.

Additionally, many senior citizens move to Mexico because the cost of assisted living is cheaper than that of assisted living facilities in the United States. Many seniors are finding it tough to live off a $1500 social security check in the United States, whereas in Mexico, $1500 a month can provide a very comfortable assisted living facility.

I reached out to a few folks that moved to Mexico from the United States to ask them about their experience so far living in a foreign country.

Michelle is fifty-five years old and has lived in Mexico for the past seven years. She currently lives in Mexicali, which is a border town with the United States, and works in the medical tourism industry.

She resides in a neighborhood of locals, in a one-bedroom home, which she pays $55 USD a month for rent. Living among the locals has allowed her to soak in the culture at the fraction of the cost of living in a large expat community. The locals have treated her very well and she said that her neighbors are "fantastic."

I asked Michelle about her experience with the healthcare system in Mexico and because she works in the medical industry, she's apt to have more insight on this topic. "I'm not fond of the public sector but the private sector is fantastic." She mentioned that many of the large pharmacy chains will have clinics where you can go with no appointment and be seen for $3–5 a visit.

HEALTHCARE

With healthcare costs skyrocketing in the United States, many folks are finding cheaper alternatives in foreign countries. Take prescription drugs, for example, don't you find it interesting that you can get prescription drugs much cheaper in our neighboring countries, Mexico and Canada, than in our own country. Often, the prices can be anywhere from 50–75 percent less expensive in Mexico and Canada. Surgical procedures are also being done in countries outside of the United States because of cost and also because some of the procedures have yet to be approved in the United States.

Many of the countries that U.S. citizens are moving to have national healthcare plans that can cover people who have a permanent visa in that country. Most of these plans are very reasonable and will cover you for minor and major medical care. Some of the plans cost $100 or less a month.

Additionally, there are U.S.-based plans that cover you in the United States as well as internationally. Obviously, this will be more expensive than getting an insurance plan with your new country, but if your new national plan does not cover outside travel, then this might be an option.

I asked her if there was anything that she would change regarding her journey to Mexico? "I would have brought more things I already owned that have electrical cords. I know that sounds odd—while the cost of living is low, anything with an electrical cord is very expensive. Fans, appliances, hair dryers…bring it with you." She mentioned that she was very happy with her life in Mexico and doubts she will return to the United States.

Jaret is forty-three years old and his wife is forty-five years old and they moved to Playa del Carmen from Canada in June 2016. He was able to retire early due to incoming rental income from owning properties. They live on less than $1000 a month. When I asked him about his experience with healthcare in Mexico, his answer: "The doctors are great! The insurance companies are difficult."

Regarding how well he is treated by the locals he said, "Mostly really well. Occasionally one will try to rip you off, but ninety-five percent of the locals are very nice and treat us well." He trains jiu-jitsu with five to six Americans, a couple of Canadians, and a few Europeans every day.

When I asked Jaret if there was anything he would change regarding his move to Mexico he said, "Nothing comes to mind. I'm very happy here." I asked what advice he would give to someone who is thinking about quitting their corporate job, selling everything, and moving to Mexico and his response: "Do it! I only wish I'd done it sooner!"

I reached out to the Expats living in Mexico Facebook page and asked them what was the main reason they picked Mexico over other countries to move to?

Here is what they said (in order of importance):

- cost of living
- people
- proximity to the United States
- culture
- weather

Many also responded that living on a monthly budget of $1500 was very doable.

Ecuador

When you start talking about retiring to another country like I have discussed in moving to Mexico, random people start throwing out names of countries they want to move to. Ecuador has come up multiple times as a destination. Ecuador sits on the Pacific Ocean, in

SAFETY FIRST

But wait, isn't Mexico supposed to be dangerous with all the drug cartels shooting up the country? Mexico gets painted with a very broad brush by the media. Are there murders and violence in Mexico due to organized crime? Absolutely, and lots of it. However, when you start digging into the stats, you'll find that a good bit of the violence is happening around the border towns of the United States and Mexico where drug trafficking is at its most intense level. Cartels battling for control create a high number of murders.

There are areas in the middle and southern parts of Mexico that are beautiful and rarely affected by the drug cartels. These areas are thousands of miles away from where most of the violence in the country is occurring.

Think of it this way, if you are a foreigner heading to the United States, all you might be hearing is everyone packs a gun and parts of the United States seem a war zone. How many foreigners have stayed away from Chicago, Detroit, and Baltimore because of how the media portrays those cities?

Whether you are looking at Mexico, Panama, Ecuador, Nicaragua, Thailand, or Vietnam, crime is everywhere. Most expats who live in these countries will tell you the same thing. Just be careful, like you would in any large U.S. city, and stay informed. Would you walk down an alley in Chicago at two in the morning? Probably not. Most expats will tell you not to drive at night, secure your purse and wallet when walking down the street, and know the areas to avoid. Use common sense, just as you would traveling around the United States.

As you explore the various countries, do your own research on the crime rates of the areas you are interested in. Again, the media misrepresents many of the stats in this area so do your own homework and contact expats living in that area to get a firsthand report.

Be aware of scams as well. In many countries, if you don't speak the language you open yourself to be targeted by scammers. It might be a cab driver who gets a kickback for talking you out of your hotel for you to stay at another hotel. In some Latin American countries, you might pay a "gringo tax" just because the merchant assumes you don't speak the language and can be taken advantage of.

The best way to avoid being scammed is to communicate with folks who already live in the country you are visiting and find out what to be on guard for. Also, knowing the language can get you out of binds as well.

the northwest corner of South America, below Columbia and above Peru. The climate can be diverse because Ecuador has coastal regions, mountainous regions, and the Amazon rainforest. There is a wet season and a dry season in Ecuador.

Why do Americans move to Ecuador? The location is beautiful, and the prices are reasonable—especially outside the tourist areas. Ecuador's currency is the U.S. dollar, so you don't have to worry about exchanging currency.

I reached out to a group of Ecuador expats and asked them what was the main reason they picked Ecuador over other countries to move to?

Here is what they said (in order of importance):

- weather
- people: "The nicest people on South American Continent."
- cost of living
- culture
- Amazon, Andes, and jungles
- freedom

I asked the group if living on $1500 a month was possible and the majority stated that it was very possible.

Costa Rica

Located between Nicaragua and Panama, Costa Rica has been a popular tourist destination for years. Many couples and individuals have visited Costa Rica, only to return home, sell all their belongings, and return to live out the rest of their lives. Because of its popularity over the years, many expats currently live in Costa Rica, so you'll be among many Americans.

Costa Rica offers beautiful beaches and rainforests plus the climate is great year-round. The healthcare system is good, and it's generally regarded as a safe country to live in. The cost to live in Costa Rica is reasonable, but it is more expensive than many of the countries in the area due to so many foreigners moving in and driving up the cost.

I reached out to a group of Costa Rica expats and asked them what was the main reason they picked Costa Rica over other countries to move to?

Here is what they said (in order of importance):

- people
- beauty and nature
- healthcare
- cost of living
- beaches

I asked the group if living on $1500 a month was possible and based on the answers it is doubtful that you could. Much like many countries, if you live in the cities and tourist areas, the cost will be higher. If you live outside of those areas, then it is possible to live under $1500 a month.

Panama

Much like Ecuador, Panama uses the U.S. dollar as its official currency although they do have their own coins, which are called balboa. Like many Central American countries, Panama offers the ability to live near the ocean or up in the mountains. You can experience the beaches on the Pacific coast or the Caribbean coast in the same day!

A lot of American influence exists in Panama as English is spoken with regularity in the cities, and they have many of the same stores you would shop at here in the states. The cost of living in Panama is higher than you might find in Mexico, but if you are looking to retire in Panama, there are benefits worth considering. Panama offers a Pensionado Program, which is open to all foreigners looking to retire there. The program gives discounts on airline tickets, entertainment, healthcare, transportation, hotels, restaurants, prescriptions, and many other benefits. This program is worth looking at if you are considering relocating to a Latin American country.

When I reached out to a group of Panama expats and asked them what the main reason was they picked Panama over other countries to move to here is what they said (in order of importance):

- weather
- cost of living
- easy to get a visa
- freedom
- healthcare
- business opportunities

When I asked the group if living on $1500 a month was possible I received mixed answers. Most of the group said no, that it would be difficult to do. Some said that it wouldn't be possible in the major cities, but if you moved out of the cities it would be doable.

Thailand

Let's now move around the globe to Southeast Asia. Thailand is a country of around 68 million people with a rapidly growing expat population. Not only are Americans moving there but also Europeans, Russians, Australians, and people from all over the world. It's a beautiful country with great beaches and wonderful culture. However, the biggest draw to Thailand for an expat is the ability to live on less than $1000. For $1000 a month, you can live comfortably in Thailand and still have money left over. Healthcare and prescription costs are very reasonable.

When choosing to live in any foreign country, you'll have to decide whether you plan to move into an expat community or live among the locals. Moving into an expat community will give you an instant network of friends, but you might find yourself living in a fishbowl—many expat communities are gated communities and you often spend more time behind the gates than immersing yourself in the local culture.

I reached out to a group of expats living in Thailand and asked them what was the main reason they picked Thailand over other countries to move to?

Here is what they said (in order of importance):

- climate
- cost of living
- people
- food
- cost of healthcare

When I asked the group if living on $1500 a month was possible the majority said yes, especially if you live in a non-tourist area.

Vietnam

Much like Thailand, Vietnam is quickly becoming an expat destination. It has tropical beaches, mountain cities, a low cost of living, and a great culture. The country is busting at the seams with people, so the infrastructure is lacking—leading to crowding in the larger cities. However, the country is investing in its infrastructure, so it is getting better.

Vietnam accepts multiple currencies such as gold, the U.S. dollar, and the Vietnam dong, which is their official currency. Like Thailand, it is very possible to live off $1000 a month in Vietnam.

As far as safety, Vietnam and Thailand are generally safe countries. Petty theft, such as pickpocketing, is common in the larger cities. Scams, such as being overcharged for services, can also happen. It really comes down to common sense. If you are walking down any street, anywhere in the world, flashing cash, then you're asking for trouble. The tourists carrying Prada bags, wearing Rolexes, with that $5000 camera around their necks are prime targets to be pickpocketed or scammed. The key is to try and look like you know what you are doing and where you are going and not call attention to yourself.

I reached out to a group of Vietnam expats and asked them what the main reason was they picked Vietnam over other countries to move to.

COMPARE COSTS

The website Numbeo (www.numbeo.com) is a great site to compare costs of various countries. You can compare cost of living, crime, healthcare, quality of life, and other statistics.

Here is a chart comparing various costs against what it would cost in the United States.

	Mexico	Ecuador	Costa Rica	Panama	Thailand	Vietnam
Meals—inexpensive restaurant	−64%	−73%	−46%	−46%	−86%	−86%
Coke/Pepsi—11.2 oz.	−64%	−54%	−16%	−38%	−67%	−74%
Water, 11.2 oz.	−64%	−65%	−8%	−30%	−79%	−80%
Domestic beer	−53%	−43%	−19%	−61%	−22%	−69%
Gasoline	35%	−29%	72%	16%	37%	21%
Levi's	−7%	57%	56%	17%	50%	−21%
Utilities (Elec./Water, Garbage for 915 sf apt.)	−76%	−75%	−52%	−53%	−54%	−62%
In-city apartment (3 bedroom)	−73%	−70%	−53%	−17%	−42%	−52%

Source: https://www.numbeo.com/cost-of-living/.

As you can see, gasoline and Levi's are more expensive in most countries. However, in every other category, significant savings can be had by moving to a foreign country.

Here is what they said (in order of importance):

- beauty of the country
- cost of beers, $1 or less (This was a popular answer. It got my attention.)
- cost of living
- good wages
- people
- food (This was mixed. Some loved the food, and some found it bland.)

When I asked the group if living on $1500 a month was possible the universal answer was absolutely. A few commented that living on $200 a month was possible, but most concurred that you could live off $500 a month and be comfortable.

How Do You Become an Expat?

First, you want to identify the country you want to move to. I'd suggest making a list of countries that appeal to you and taking some scouting trips to narrow down your list. I'd also suggest connecting with expat groups on Facebook to ask questions and get their opinions on specific locations within the countries you are interested in.

You'll want to determine whether you plan on renting or buying a home in your new country. My advice is to rent for a year or two to be sure this is where you plan your permanent home will be. Many of the popular expat locations are littered with homes that wealthy Americans purchased or built and then, several years later, decided to move back to the United States. They have found that it's not as easy to sell the home as it is back in the states.

Once you have identified the location you plan to move to, you're going to want to see what the requirements are for a permanent resident visa, which allows you to live in that country. A visa is an official document that allows you to stay in a country for a specific period. There are some visas that allow for a short-term visit for a month up to generally ninety days. These are referred to as tourist visas. If you plan on moving to a foreign country, then you will want to research what it takes to qualify for a permanent resident visa. The qualifications will vary depending on the country. Some countries require that you prove you have a certain amount of income to live there full-time. Some countries offer incentives to move there, such as Panama and their *pensionado* residency program. Many of the countries we discussed are what we would call emerging markets, which means they are experiencing growth, but they still have a poorer population. Many will have a financial requirement because they don't want you coming in and running out of money.

Once your visa is approved, start learning about the culture, the local laws, learn the language, and start thinking about what possessions you plan on selling off and which ones you plan on taking with you.

Check with your local bank to see if your debit and credit cards will work in the country you are moving to. Get familiar with the currency exchange. Open a bank account in your new country. Find the ATMs around your new location because, as they always say, "Cash is king."

Ask your CPA or accountant if they are comfortable dealing with someone living in a foreign country especially if you plan on working in your new location. Some tax preparers might not be too comfortable with the ins and outs of foreign tax laws.

Make sure you get your health insurance in order before you leave the United States. Do you plan on keeping your U.S.-based plan or do you plan on signing up for your new country's healthcare plan? Decide on this ahead of time.

Check with your cell phone carrier to see if you can get a plan that will cover you in your new country until you can get to your new location and switch over to a local plan.

Start accepting that your world is getting ready to change. Things are going to be different than you are used to. In the United States, we might make an appointment for a repair person to show up between a three-hour window on a certain day. In a foreign country, a repair person will show when they want to show, perhaps a week later, so be prepared for a slower pace.

ON THE MOVE

This is a perfect time to start getting rid of all that stuff you don't need or use anymore. If you plan on packing up your whole house in the United States and moving it to another country, then this lifestyle might not be for you. Yes, take the important items, but trying to bring your whole home to say, Costa Rica, might be a bit much—plus ungodly expensive to do.

My home is 2100 square feet and 90 percent of it is just unnecessary to me. Yes, I need a sofa and some chairs and the regular stuff that everyone else needs in their home but what do we really need? I want to get to the point that everything I need is in one backpack or suitcase. I pretty much wear the same seven or eight things each week anyway. So, if I throw those things in a backpack, along with my laptop and my bathroom kit, I'm ready to go.

Action Plan

You don't have to be a millionaire to retire early. Some people believe you must have extraordinary wealth to be able to retire when you are forty-five to fifty-five years old. I've shared six countries (and there are many more) where you could retire and live comfortably for under $1500 a month and, in some cases, under $1000 a month. It's not for everyone, many of you may still have family obligations in the United States that you might not want to be too far from. But if you are seeking freedom, a change of pace, adventure, and less financial stress, moving to another country and becoming an expat might be for you.

Sure, you might have to bring your job with you, work remotely, or maybe you don't work because you have saved enough to never work again. Instead of renting that coastal villa on the beach in Mexico, you might need to rent one three blocks from the ocean. There will be sacrifices, but aren't you sacrificing your health right now if you are in a stressful career?

In emerging countries, be prepared for it to be different from the United States. For example, while driving down the road, you might have to stop for a random cow to cross the street. You may have the driver in front of you stop in the middle of a busy street to hold a conversation with his buddy. The pace in most countries is slower than the United States, but isn't that what you are looking for? In the United States we drive fast, eat fast, talk fast, and live our lives in fast forward. I believe all of us are looking to slow down and enjoy our time. By moving to a foreign country that looks at life and living different than we do in the United States, it will force you to slow down, which isn't necessarily a terrible thing.

What is great about expat living is that you can define it and shape it how you desire. Some expats will fall in love with one country and decide to move there full-time, whereas others will move around from country to country.

Don't be scared. Here lies your challenge: Get out there and see the world before it's too late. Millions of Americans live around the world right now and you can be one of them. Explore a rainforest, see the Mayan Ruins, drink a guaro sour on the beach in Costa Rica. See what your options are—you might fall in love with an area and decide to move there. If you do, your life will never be the same.

AFTERWORD

I started the process of writing this book with the thought of working two to three more years as a financial advisor. As the book progressed, so did my thoughts of retiring now versus waiting. I sold my financial advising firm and I'm happy to report that I am now retired at age forty-eight. I'm still in the very early stage so it feels rather odd not going to the office every day. My thoughts are slowing down, and I feel like I have time to think again rather than have my mind filled with constant work-related items.

How did I successfully pull off early retirement? I must have sold my advising firm for millions or had some inheritance to fall back on, right? Wrong. I've never been given anything or inherited any money. I worked very hard for every dollar I made. Regarding my advising firm, I think you would be surprised at just how little I got for it.

I will work, but I'll work on *my* terms. I'll work when I want, how I want, and from where I want. I am finally in control of my own freedom.

With two teenagers, my travels will be limited for the next two and half years. My plan is to visit Mexico, Ecuador, Costa Rica, Panama, Nicaragua and other areas on quick scouting trips to figure out where

I want to spend more time in the future. There will also be trips in our RV here and there. Follow along with me on my blog (http://www.retireearly365.com/blog) to read about my adventures.

Once the kids are away to college, my week trips can now become monthlong trips. I can't wait until we can spend a month in the Arizona desert in January or a month in Thailand. My kids will be popping in and out at home, so while they are in college, I plan on keeping my home until college is wrapped up. Once they're done with college, I should have a very clear picture of where I want to live. It might be in Mexico or Ecuador, perhaps a small secluded cabin in Montana or a mobile lifestyle that keeps me moving around.

I plan to continue helping people find their own freedom and think differently about their own retirement. Right now, my website is up and running (www.retireearly365.com), and I envision a YouTube channel, workshops, and a possible podcast. My goal is to help people think independently about retirement and not just go with what society expects.

Stay tuned for the next book.

If you need help planning your own early retirement, you can go to www.retireearly365.com and see a few different packages available where I can help you chart your course. I no longer give specific investment advice or manage money because I'm retired. These packages are based on helping you get your whole financial life in order, as well as helping hold you accountable to achieve your freedom.

Remember, it's up to you to take control of your own life and be free. What are you waiting for?

See you on the road….

Eric Gaddy
Spring 2018

INDEX

ABOUT THE AUTHOR

ERIC GADDY retired at age forty-eight after twenty-four years as a financial advisor. Eric's financial advising career took him from training in NYC with Dean Witter to residing in Asheville, NC, for the past twenty-two years.

Over his twenty-four-year career, Eric met with over 8000 individuals and couples, helping them successfully navigate to and through retirement. During his career, he was a retirement planning expert and a Chartered Retirement Planning Counselor (CRPC). In 2010, Eric formed his own wealth firm, Ethos Wealth Group, which he sold in the fall of 2017.

Growing up, Eric was raised in the mortuary business, which might explain his rather different sense of humor. However, it instilled in him that "Life is short" from the very beginning. Eric is very aware of his own mortality, which is one of the main reasons, combined with his financial advising career, that he wrote this book.

Eric can be contacted at www.retireearly365.com.

BE SURE TO GRAB YOUR
COPY OF THE ACCOMPANYING
WORKBOOK
AND GET STARTED ON YOUR
ROAD TO EARLY FREEDOM!

- Section by Section questions and answers to help you get clear on your financial position
- Organized DIAL™ system for you to follow to know where to take action
- Results pages to get your real numbers for Retiring Early

Eric Gaddy also offers DIAL into Early Retirement™ Coaching Packages to truly assist you as you move through the Workbook and far beyond. He can answer questions, help you map scenarios, and give you tips you won't hear anywhere else.

THE WORKBOOK, COACHING, FREE BLOGS,
AND MUCH MORE CAN BE FOUND AT THE HOME SITE!

www.RetireEarly365.com